BEYOND
NOSE
TO
TAIL

First published in Great Britain 2007

Copyright © 2007 by Fergus Henderson
and Justin Piers Gellatly
Photographs copyright © 2007 by Jason Lowe

The moral right of the authors has been asserted

Bloomsbury Publishing Plc,
36 Soho Square, London W1D 3QY

A CIP catalogue record for this book is available
from the British Library

ISBN 9780747589143
10 9 8 7 6 5 4 3 2 1

Designed by willwebb.co.uk
The text of this book is set in Sabon

Printed and bound in Italy by L.E.G.O.

The paper this book is printed on is certified by the © 1996 Forest
Stewardship Council A. C. (FSC). It is ancient-forest friendly.
The printer holds FSC chain of custody SGS-COC-2939

FSC
Mixed Sources
Product group from well-managed
forests and other controlled sources

Cert no. SGS-COC-2939
www.fsc.org
© 1996 Forest Stewardship Council

www.bloomsbury.com/fergushenderson

BEYOND
NOSE
TO
TAIL

A KIND
OF BRITISH
COOKING:
PART II

FERGUS
HENDERSON
&
JUSTIN PIERS
GELLATLY

PHOTOGRAPHS BY
JASON LOWE

BLOOMSBURY

FH

For Brian and Elizabeth Henderson

JPG

For Louise, my wonderful wife

FOUR MORE THINGS I THOUGHT
IT MIGHT BE WORTH MENTIONING

Nose to Tail Eating was admittedly short on the world of puddings, baking and bread, but we now have a chance to correct that failing with the aid of Justin Piers Gellatly, my pastry chef and head baker, who has spread his pastry wings and taken us beyond Nose to Tail.

The perfect recipe manages to steady and uplift at the same time.

One afternoon my flat was broken into. The strange thing is, before I went out I had put a hare in the oven to braise, which filled the flat with delicious gamey smells. I cannot help but think that it must have been very distracting to the burglar, the musk of a braising hare.

Unctuous potential: Trotter Gear is your gastronomic friend.

CONTENTS

PIG'S HEAD

TROTTER GEAR

PUDDINGS

STEADYING PUDDINGS

ICE CREAM

SOMETHING TO GET THE JUICES GOING

CAMPARI AND WHITE WINE

Having ended my last book on a cure for overindulgence, I thought, on a positive note, we should start this book on something to lead you into your indulgence, a cleansing glass to get the juices going. It's known in Italy as a bicyclette, as old men drink it and then wobble home on their bikes. Interestingly, Harry's Bar in Venice refuses to serve this concoction, rather as if it's Italy's version of a snakebite, but do not be deterred.

In a wineglass pour a measure of Campari, add some ice and top up with dry white wine. With trial and error, you shall find your chosen strength.

Your good health and appetite!

PIG SKIN AND FAT

SALTED BACK FAT AND WET WALNUTS

Rather like eating grown-up peanut butter.

Take a piece of pork back fat (the Middle White pig has a good layer) and cover it with sea salt. Leave it in the fridge for a month. When its time is up, brush the salt off and slice very thinly on to a plate.

Crack your walnuts open and extract the nuts. Break into pieces over the plated back fat.

Eat with fingers, rolling the back fat around some walnut and popping it in your mouth.

PORK SCRATCHINGS,
A VERSION OF

*pig's skin
(ask your butcher),
with some fat attached*

sea salt

*enough duck fat
to cover the skin*

A most steadying nibble.

Spread a layer of sea salt on a plastic tray, or anything that won't react with the salt. Lay the skin on top and sprinkle liberally with sea salt. Leave in the fridge for 5 days.

When its time is up, remove the skin from the fridge and soak overnight in cold water. Rinse in clean water. Thoroughly dry with a clean tea towel and lay it in an oven tray. Cover with duck fat, then cover the tray with foil. Cook in a medium oven for 2½ hours. As with all things cooking, keep an eye on it.

Take it out of the oven and allow to cool, smearing it with the solidifying duck fat. At this point you can keep it in the fridge until your next drinks party, or a frail moment when you are in need of such nourishment.

When such a moment arrives, place a rack on an oven tray, then lay your skin on top. Again put into a medium oven, in which it should slightly puff up into a sheet of golden, crispy joy (be careful not to brown it, as this is bitter and sad). Now remove from the oven and allow to cool. Place the crispy skin on a board and chop it with a heavy knife. It should break up into pieces. Serve.

A word of warning, though: with fragile dental arrangements, eat with caution.

SOUP

(Never underestimate the power of Soup)

FENNEL, BUTTER BEAN,
OX TONGUE AND GREEN SAUCE

Makes a pot that will do a hearty lunch for six

1 ox tongue, brined for 10–14 days (see page 208)

a few stock vegetables, such as carrot, leek, celery, onion, garlic, roughly chopped

olive oil

6 heads of fennel, sliced thinly against the grain

4 firm white onions, peeled and sliced 3mm thick

8 cloves of garlic, peeled and left whole

1 small glass of Pernod

chicken stock

A lot going on for a soup, but what a soup!

Rinse the brined ox tongue and soak it for a couple of hours in fresh water. Put it in a pan with the stock vegetables, bring to the boil and simmer for 3 hours. Check with a knife; you want a thoroughly giving tongue. Peel it while still warm, then allow to cool.

We are almost ready to construct our soup … In a pot big enough to receive all the ingredients, pour a healthy splash of olive oil and put on a not too furious heat. Sweat off the fennel, onions and garlic until giving but not collapsing, as they still have some cooking to do. Add the Pernod.

At this point, add enough chicken stock to cover everything, then add the butter beans. What you want is beans *in* the soup, not a thick, beany soup. Think of the Mysterons of Captain Scarlet, and the circles of light that came with them – that's the sort of bean ratio you are looking for in the soup. Let this simmer, allowing all the components to get to know each other.

2 handfuls of butter beans, soaked overnight and then simmered thoroughly in clean water with a head of garlic, until they are soft, swollen pillows of joy (very important, as we know what happens to undercooked beans – nothing!)

Green Sauce (see page 211)

sea salt and black pepper

Now slice as much tongue as you feel appropriate (keep the rest for sandwiches) into thin little angel's wings. Slip these into the soup. After a moment's more introductory simmering, check for seasoning and serve with a big bowl of green sauce to dollop, plus bread and wine.

A fine lunch.

NETTLE AND SNAIL SOUP

To serve six

4 floury potatoes, peeled and chopped into chunks

4 leeks, cleaned and sliced

2 onions, peeled and sliced

4 cloves of garlic, peeled and chopped

olive oil

1.5 litres light chicken stock

a good shopping bag full of nettles

sea salt and black pepper

This should be made with spring nettles, as by July they tend to take on a laxative quality. Probably not what you want from a soup.

In a saucepan sweat off all your chopped vegetables in olive oil, not browning them. This moment is important, as the more you can cook the vegetables at this point, the better the flavour of the soup. When the potatoes are cooked, add the stock. Let this all simmer, familiarising the elements.

While still simmering away on the heat, add the nettles. Allow them to blanch for a moment – not long enough to lose their vivid green – then take off the heat and liquidise the lot.

At this point it might have a certain rustic, fibrous nature. Do not worry – you now need to pass the soup through a fine sieve twice, as eradicating any fibre somehow spiritually defeats the nettles by removing any fear of a tingle or a sting. You now hopefully have a green, silky soup.

SNAILS

24 fresh English snails, picked by your fair hands (you will need to put them in a bucket and let them poo all their poo out for a few days before cooking; then blanch in boiling salt water, pull them out of their shells and cook in a court-bouillon – that is, water with plenty of white wine and flavoursome herbs – until tender); or there is Tony the Snail Man, who breeds snails (see right)

12 cloves of garlic, peeled and finely chopped

a big knob of butter

Address your snails: pop the chopped garlic and butter into a heated frying pan. Allow for a little sizzle, then add the snails. Roll them around until piping hot, then season with salt and pepper.

Bowl up the nettle soup and spoon in 4 snails per person, which should stay on the top, sitting in a buttery, garlicky puddle.

P.S. Tony the Snail Man said I could give you his number, 01432 760218, and he might be able to sort you out, depending on where you are.

POTATO AND BACK FAT SOUP

To serve six

12 floury potatoes (this
is important as we are
aiming at liquid silk, not
wallpaper paste), peeled
and chopped

6 leeks, cleaned
and chopped

5 onions, peeled
and chopped

10 cloves of garlic,
peeled and chopped

olive oil

1 litre light chicken stock

1 litre milk

sea salt and black pepper

TOPPING

125g salted back fat (as
with the wet walnuts, on
page 6, but cut into
baked-bean-sized
chunks)

OR

6 healthy slices of
fresh foie gras

The ultimate soothing yet steadying soup; if feeling a little liverish, or generally frail, this should sort you out.

As with the previous recipe, sweat off all the chopped vegetables in a pan with the oil. Again I cannot stress enough how much more improved the flavour of the soup will be the longer you can extend this moment. The perfect result would be the potatoes completely cooked (leaving no glimmer of the bitterness of raw potato).

Add the stock and milk and simmer away until all the vegetables have given up any sign of resistance. Put through a fine sieve. Check for seasoning.

Now you have various options; eat the soup as is, which might seem a bit dour. Or, in a frying pan, render your small chunks of salted back fat on not too high a heat, so that you end up with crispy nuduals of salty pork fat to top off the soup. But our possibilities do not end there. You could instead sear off a generous slice of fresh foie gras per bowl of soup, pop on top of the hot soup and give it a few minutes to do a little melting, then eat.

VEAL TAIL AND PEA SOUP

To serve four

veal bones, roasted in a hot oven for half an hour

stock vegetables – carrot, leek, celery, onion, garlic – roughly chopped

a bundle of herbs – parsley, thyme, a little rosemary

2 veal tails per person, brined for at least a week (see page 208), then a good soak in fresh water overnight to desalinate

900g fresh peas in their pods, podded just before use – or you could apply the theory a wise chef once told me, which was to use fresh when peas are in season and otherwise use frozen

sea salt and black pepper

This is a perfect case of why you must befriend your butchers and give them a bit of advance warning. They should be able to get you the tails. If they come in dribs and drabs, get your brine bucket out and use it as a holding tank until you have amassed enough tails.

Put the roasted veal bones, chopped stock vegetables and bundle of herbs into a pot. Place the tails on top, cover with water and simmer for 3 hours, skimming as you go. Then, making sure that the tails are thoroughly cooked, with a sharp knife, remove gently and put to one side.

Strain the broth and chill it thoroughly. Clarify the broth as described on page 209. Return to the heat and check the seasoning. Reintroduce the tails and, at the last moment, add the peas and serve.

Encourage the use of fingers in the picking up of the tails and giving them a good gnaw. This soup is a thing of beauty, with tails and peas bobbing about in a clear broth ... Ahhh.

SALADS

(Be firm but fair with salads)

BACON, EGG AND BEAN SALAD

thinly sliced yesterday's pot-roast bacon

7-minute boiled eggs, 1½ per person (one of those situations where 1 seems mean, but 2 too much)

green beans, topped and tailed, then cooked in boiling salted water until bendy but not soft

Vinaigrette (see page 210)

lots of chopped curly parsley

Excuse the rather tongue-in-cheek reference to the great national dish.

This is an ideal way to use up leftover pot-roast bacon (see page 43), so it will serve as many as your leftover bacon allows.

Mix all together in a bowl, add bread, wine and friends – the perfect lunch.

BREAD & WINE SALAD

To serve four

5 *Little Gem lettuces,*
cleaned and cut across
at 1cm intervals

4 *spring onions, finely*
sliced across

a sprig or two of
mint, chopped

juice of ½ lemon

a modest splash of
red wine vinegar

a healthy splash of
extra virgin olive oil

sea salt and black pepper

The disciplining of vegetables is not to be taken lightly. Letting them know you are in charge is one thing but full-on chopping is another. This salad, created for St. John Bread & Wine, is an example of extreme rigour applied to a Little Gem lettuce.

Mix all together in a bowl. Enjoy the discipline.

BUTTER BEAN, LEEK AND CAULIFLOWER SALAD

To serve four to six

2 handfuls of
butter beans

2 heads of garlic

1 happy head of
cauliflower, taken
apart into challenging
bite-sized florets

4 leeks, sliced across at
5mm intervals, then
thoroughly rinsed

a bunch of curly parsley,
finely chopped

a handful of
extra-fine capers

DRESSING

300ml extra virgin olive
oil – it's a thirsty salad

juice of 1 juicy or 2 not
so juicy lemons

6 cloves of garlic, peeled
and thoroughly crushed
(this may seem a lot, but
remember the dressing
has to bring 'wayhay'
to some very calm
elements)

sea salt and black pepper

Unusually for a salad, this enjoys sitting, getting to know its dressing. It is inspired by Ellen Hooberman, a master of the caper, garlic and chopped parsley, which is a good thing!

Soak the butter beans overnight in cold water, then drain and cook in clean water with the heads of garlic – this can take 2 to 3 hours – so that you have your aforementioned pillows of joy (see page 13).

Whisk all the dressing ingredients together thoroughly, adding salt and pepper to taste.

Take the cauliflower and butter beans and liberally dress them. Toss and then leave to sit overnight.

When it comes time to serve, just tease the leeks for a moment in some boiling salted water. The warmth of the leek, added to the cauliflower and butter beans, should awaken the slumbering salad. Once awake, it may need some more dressing – take a view. Add the chopped parsley and a substantial handful of capers. Toss vigorously, being careful not to crush the butter beans, then serve.

BEETROOT, RED ONION, RED CABBAGE, CRÈME FRAÎCHE AND CHERVIL

To serve six

2 *raw beetroot, peeled and finely grated*

¼ *raw red cabbage with its core cut out, very finely sliced*

1 *small red onion, peeled, cut in half from top to bottom and finely sliced*

6 *healthy dollops of crème fraîche*

2 *healthy bunches of chervil, picked*

DRESSING

healthy splashes of extra virgin olive oil

a little gesture of balsamic vinegar

a small handful of extra-fine capers

sea salt and black pepper

Too often you are offered a *fait accompli* on a plate, a weave of ingredients in which your only involvement will be to make a mess of it, with the inevitable intervention of your knife and fork. Well, here is a salad that welcomes the messing-up process.

Mix everything together for the dressing. Toss all your raw red vegetables in the dressing, then on six plates place a bushel of this red mixture. Next to this, nustle your blob of crème fraîche as if the two ingredients were good friends, not on top of each other as if they were lovers. Finally a clump of the chervil rested next to the other ingredients in the friendly fashion.

A very striking salad ready for the eater to mess up.

WHITE CABBAGE AND BROWN SHRIMP

To serve six

½ *standard white cabbage, very thinly sliced – you will be surprised by how much you have once the cabbage is chopped (there is also the gas factor to remember when eating raw cabbage; I think there is only so much the tummy can take)*

2 handfuls of peeled brown shrimps (Morecambe Bay)

2 bunches of chervil, 1 chopped finely (for flavour) and the other picked (for the salad's glamour)

DRESSING

juice of 1 lemon

extra virgin olive oil

sea salt and black pepper

This is a wonderful salad.

It is as simple as mixing all the ingredients together so you end up with the little brown shrimps caught in a weave of cabbage. The salty sweetness of the shrimp makes a happy companion to the mysterious warmth of the raw cabbage.

KOHLRABI

I don't think this should be a recipe but more a moment of celebration for this rather unutilised member of the cabbage family, which comes across as more of a root, with a kind of appley turnip quality.

Peeled and sliced thinly, it makes a great addition to a salad – in fact on its own with chervil, capers, lemon and extra virgin olive oil makes for a delicious crunchy salad. Add some finely shaved fennel or chicory – anyway, now I've made the introduction, it's Liberty Hall.

PIG'S HEAD

PRESSED PIG'S EAR

To serve eight to ten as a starter

14 *pig's ears, cleaned and any remaining hair shaved off with a Bic razor, then brined for at least 3 days (see page 208)*

3 *pig's trotters, cleaned*

2 *onions, peeled*

2 *carrots, peeled*

2 *leeks, cleaned*

2 *sticks of celery*

a head of garlic

a bundle of parsley, thyme and rosemary

2 *bay leaves*

peppercorns

enough very light chicken stock to cover the above ingredients

This is as close as it gets to turning a sow's ear into a silk purse. One could be forgiven for thinking of ears as rubbery things, not blessed with much culinary potential. Well, think again!

Pig's ears are not expensive so don't be shy; ask your butcher, who should have no problem getting them, as where there are pigs there must be ears. If you have to amass your ears over a few days, do not worry, as this is where your brine bucket will come in handy.

Remove the ears from the brine, rinse thoroughly and soak in fresh water for half a day. Final ear procedure: you need to flatten them, so when they turn into funnels split them open with a knife.

Place all the ingredients in a pot and cover with the chicken stock, then lid on pot and into a medium oven for 4 hours. After 3 hours, take a look; remember you want a totally submissive texture, but also that there is the cartilage in the ear, which will never give in.

When done, remove from the oven. Carefully take out the ears and layer them in a terrine mould or bread tin lined with cling film. Strain the liquor off the vegetables and trotters into a clean pan. Place on the hob and simmer until reduced to the point where it will still cover the ears. Check for seasoning – remember it is going to be served cold, which always dulls flavour.

Pour the reduced liquor over the ears. Cut a bit of cardboard to fit in your mould, cover it with cling film and place on top of your juicy ears. Apply weights to it – tins of tomato etc. Allow to cool, then leave in the fridge overnight. Next day it is ready to eat.

Turn the pressed pig's ears out of the container and slice very thinly with a very sharp knife. What you should have now is thin slivers of joyous piggy jelly, within which there is a beautiful weave of ear. When you bite into it, you should have that splendid textural moment of the give of the jelly and the slightest crunch of the ear cartilage. Serve with cornichons.

CONFIT PIG'S CHEEK AND DANDELION

To serve four

4 pig's cheeks

*a handful of
coarse sea salt*

duck or goose fat

*12 shallots, peeled
and left whole*

*12 cloves of garlic,
peeled and left whole*

4 slices of good bread

*a bunch of
dandelion leaves*

*a handful of
extra-fine capers*

*a bunch of parsley,
finely chopped*

*Vinaigrette
(see page 210)*

A dish that could be accused of being a salad, but I see it more as lunch.

Ask your butcher for pig's cheeks; you need the skin and fat on, not just the nuggets of flesh. This should not be too difficult, given a day or two's warning.

Salt your cheeks and leave overnight. Next day, brush them off thoroughly with a clean kitchen cloth, then lay them in a deepish oven dish and cover with duck or goose fat. Cover with foil and pop them into a gentle to medium oven for approximately 3 hours. Keep an eye on them; you want a giving cheek when stabbed with a sharp knife. When happy with the stabbing, remove them from the oven and allow to cool in the fat. At this point you could keep the cheeks covered in the fat in the fridge for a rainy day or proceed by removing them from the fat. Scrape off any excess with your fingers and keep the fat for future use.

Don't forget your shallots and garlic. Put them in an ovenproof dish, cover with duck or goose fat and roast until soft, sweet and giving.

Place the slices of bread in an ovenproof dish, on top of which you should rest your cheeks. Slip it into a medium oven and allow the cheeks to loosen up, the fat to crisp up and the bread to absorb all the goodness – about 1½ hours.

When the cheeks are crispy, you are ready. Place the dandelion leaves in a bowl with the shallots, garlic, capers and parsley. Then lay your bread and cheeks on a board and chop into spirited chunks with a heavy knife. Add them to your leaves of dandelion. Dress. Toss with conviction, open the red wine and away you go ...

PIG'S HEAD AND BEANS

Should feed approximately six

1 pig's head – remove any unwanted hair with a Bic razor

2 carrots, peeled

2 onions, cut in half

2 heads of garlic

2 sticks of celery

2 leeks, slit in half lengthways and cleaned

a handful of black peppercorns

zest of 1 lemon

a splash of red wine vinegar

½ bottle of white wine

The wobble of pig's head, the starchy give of beans, the slight crunch of vegetable and the naagh of red wine vinegar, it's all there.

Place the head in a large pot with the vegetables, peppercorns, lemon zest, vinegar and wine. Cover with water, bring to a gentle boil, then reduce to a simmer. Cook for 3–4 hours, skimming as you go, until the head is totally giving and coming away easily from the bone.

Remove the head and leave until cool enough to handle, then take the meat from the skull (don't forget the tongue). Meanwhile, strain the cooking liquor into a clean pan and reserve.

*2 handfuls of fresh
borlotti beans, cooked in
clean water with 2 heads
of garlic*

*6 carrots, cut into long,
thin slices with a peeler*

*a bunch of spring
onions, cut into 1cm
sections*

*a bunch of radishes,
trimmed, but keep the
leaves if happy*

*2 bunches of watercress,
stalks chopped off*

*a healthy splash of red
wine vinegar*

sea salt and black pepper

Cut the meat into walnut-sized chunks and return them to the pan of cooking liquor. Add the beans and allow them to bond emotionally but not physically on the heat. When you feel there is the appropriate rapport between head and beans, add the other ingredients, seasoning to taste with salt, pepper and the vinegar. Allow your vegetables time to wilt but not cook, so that you have the wobble of head with the gentle resistance of the wilting veg and the reassuring bean element, all captured in a puddle on the plate. Serve immediately.

POT-ROAST HALF PIG'S HEAD

To serve two

a dollop of duck fat

8 shallots, peeled and left whole

8 cloves of garlic, peeled and left whole

½ pig's head (your butcher should have no problems supplying this) – remove any hairs with a razor

a glass of brandy

1 bundle of joy – thyme, parsley and a little rosemary

½ bottle of white wine

chicken stock

a healthy spoonful of Dijon mustard

1 bunch of watercress, trimmed, or other greens – a case of Liberty Hall

sea salt and black pepper

I say only half a head, as it is a perfect romantic supper for two. Imagine gazing into the eyes of your loved one over a golden pig's cheek, ear and snout.

Dollop the duck fat into an oven tray wide and deep enough to accommodate your half a pig's head and put it on the heat. Add the shallots and garlic and leave them to do a little sweating to improve the flavour of the dish. Shuggle the tin occasionally to prevent any burning, but you do want some colour.

When happy with these, cover the ear of your demi-head with foil so that it doesn't frazzle, then rest the head in the tin. To welcome it to its new environment, pour the glass of brandy over it, nustle in your bundle of joy, add the wine and then the chicken stock. Now, I'm sure we have covered this before – the alligator-in-the-swamp theory – what we are looking for is the half pig's head to lurk in the stock in a not dissimilar fashion to an alligator in a swamp.

Season with salt and pepper, cover the tin with grease-proof paper, offering some protection but not denying the need for the rigours of the hours to come in the oven – which is where you should now put your tin, in a medium oven for 3 hours, until the head is totally giving. Check it after 2–2½ hours; you could remove the greaseproof paper at this point and get a little colour on your cheek.

When ready, remove the head to a warm place. Whisk the Dijon mustard into the pan liquor, in which you should then wilt the bunch of watercress.

Finally, on the head presentation platter, make a pillow of shallots, garlic and wilted watercress, where you then rest your head. There you have it, dinner for two; open something red and delicious: Moon, June, Spoon.

St. JOHN

TROTTER GEAR

UNCTUOUS POTENTIAL

TROTTER GEAR

(Unctuous potential)

RECIPE FOR A HEALTHY JAR
OF TROTTER GEAR

Makes one healthy jar

*6 pig's trotters, all hair
removed (a disposable
Bic razor can prove very
useful at this moment)*

2 onions, peeled

2 carrots, peeled

2 sticks of celery

*2 leeks, slit in half
lengthways and cleaned*

1 head of garlic

a bundle of thyme

a handful of peppercorns

½ bottle Sercial Madeira

*enough chicken stock to
cover the trotters*

Alluded to in the previous book, but not fully fledged, it now has a name and a place in every kitchen. This unctuous, giving gastronomic tool will become all chefs' and cooks' friend, finding untold uses in the kitchen. No fridge should be without its jar of Trotter Gear.

Place the trotters in a large casserole. Cover with water and bring to the boil. Boil for 5 minutes, then drain. This removes the initial scum given off by the trotters.

Now place the blanched trotters back in the pot with the vegetables, thyme, peppercorns and Madeira and cover with stock. Cover and place in a gentle oven. Cook for at least 3 hours, until the trotters are totally giving. At this point, strain the cooking liquor and keep. When the trotters have cooled enough to handle (but don't let them go cold, as they become much harder to deal with), pick all the flesh, fat and skin off them, tearing the skin into shreds. Add to the cooking liquor, seal in a jar and refrigerate.

You now have Trotter Gear, nuduals of giving, wobbly trotter captured in a splendid jelly. One can sense its potential even now.

POT-ROAST BACON,
TROTTER AND PRUNE

To serve six

2 *white onions,*
peeled and sliced

a dollop of duck fat

1 *piece of smoked bacon*
loin (Gloucester Old
Spot does very well)
– cut the skin off in one
piece and keep

500g *Trotter Gear*
(see left)

a large glass of
white wine

22 *Agen prunes,*
stones in

chicken stock up
your sleeve, in case a
top-up is needed

black pepper

This is a firm favourite. With these ingredients, how can you go wrong? Also, leftovers are good.

In a deep oven tray big enough to hold all your ingredients, sweat the onions in the duck fat until slightly softened. Place the bacon on the feathered nest, surround with Trotter Gear, and add the wine, prunes, pepper and any top-up of stock needed so that the bacon is almost covered. Lay the skin back on the bacon like a protective duvet, cover in foil and put into a medium oven for 1¾–2 hours, keeping an eye on it to make sure nothing too ferocious is happening to it.

When ready, the prunes should have swollen with pride but maintained their dignity, thanks to their stones. Slice the bacon and serve with a hearty spoonful of trotter, onion and prune. What a joy!

DEEP-FRIED RABBIT

To serve four

2 young wild rabbits,
jointed (2 shoulders,
2 saddle sections and
2 back legs each)

500g Trotter Gear
(see page 42)

chicken stock, to top up

seasoned flour

egg wash (an egg beaten
with a tiny splash of
milk), with a spoonful
of Dijon mustard
whisked in

very fine breadcrumbs
(the fineness is important
so that you do not
end up with a bready
layer between you and
your rabbit)

vegetable oil for
deep-frying

lemons, cut in half

This dish is improved by the use of rabbits with youth on their side. So if you have a friend with a gun, ask them to aim for the smaller bunnies.

A deep-fat fryer is very handy for this recipe, but a pan of hot vegetable oil will suffice.

Place the jointed rabbit in a casserole, cover with the Trotter Gear and stock and place a lid or foil over the top. Put in a gentle oven. Cook for 2 hours but as always, check with a sharp knife. I cannot stress *gentle* enough – you should have a submissive rabbit after its time, safely submerged in protective Trotter Gear. Remove the rabbit but keep the Trotter Gear, which at this point has huge flavoursome, unctuous potential.

When the rabbit is cool, dust in the seasoned flour, coat in the mustardy egg wash and then a fine layer of breadcrumbs. Deep-fry until golden. Place on kitchen paper to drain off the fat and then serve in a bowl from which everyone helps themselves, with lemon and a glass or two of something red and chirpy.

BACON, TROTTER AND PRUNE ON FOIE GRAS TOAST

Sometimes great things come out of moments of adversity. At St. John Bread & Wine a foie gras terrine had not turned out as happy as we would have wished but, always thinking on one's feet, we had the leftovers of bacon, prune and trotter ...

Basic foie advice: Pull the lobes of one fresh duck's foie apart with your fingers and remove the veins. Then splash on a spot of Vieille Prune (or eau de vie of choice), toss well and cover. Pop in the fridge overnight.

Next day, get a clean Kilner jar, season your foie well with salt and toss again. Then press it into the jar, which you sit on a folded tea towel in an ovenproof dish. Surround the jar with water, lid open. Don't let any water into the jar. Place carefully in a gentle oven and keep a close eye on it. Fat will be released, which is good, but do not let your foie melt away. When happy with the state of things, remove the jar from its bath. Remember it will carry on cooking. Add the rubber seal and shut, as simple as that. When cold, pop it into the fridge.

Chop a bit of the bacon into chunks and add to the prunes and trotters. Heat up in a pan. When hot, pour the mixture over a piece of toast on which you have spread the foie gras.

You could not wish for a more steadying, but at the same time uplifting, snack.

GUINEA FOWL, RED CABBAGE, TROTTER AND PRUNE

Each guinea fowl will feed two to three people, depending on their appetite

1 guinea fowl – you can expand this recipe exponentially

duck fat

1 red onion, peeled and sliced

about ½ red cabbage, thinly sliced (enough to make a small nest for the bird)

4 cloves of garlic, peeled and left whole

500g Trotter Gear (see page 42)

14 Agen prunes

a bundle of thyme

2 bay leaves

2 large glasses of red wine

chicken stock, to cover

sea salt and black pepper

A most comforting sight in the middle of the table, happy bird surrounded by red cabbage, wobbly trotter and prunes.

Guinea fowl could be replaced by pheasant with equally delicious results. In fact, come the winter, all the more appropriate.

Brown off your bird in duck fat, in a pan or oven tray. When appropriately tanned, remove the bird and soften the onion in the fat. Add the cabbage and garlic. Stuff the bird with some Trotter Gear and a few prunes.

Nustle the stuffed bird upside down in the cabbage and add the remaining Trotter Gear and prunes, plus the bundle of thyme, bay leaves, red wine, salt and pepper. Cover the cabbage with chicken stock. Cover the oven tray with foil and slip it into a gentle oven for 2½ hours – as always, keeping an eye on it. Check with a knife to see if you have a giving bird.

I sometimes worry about my bacon count, but this braise would happily welcome the addition of a chunk of smoked bacon.

BEEF AND PICKLED WALNUT STEW

To serve two

1 flap off a fore rib

4 red onions, peeled and sliced

5 cloves of garlic, peeled and left whole

a bundle of thyme and rosemary

½ bottle of red wine

500g Trotter Gear (see page 42)

8 pickled walnuts

sea salt and black pepper

This is a treat for the chef who has prepared a fore rib for Sunday lunch. If you take the flap off the rib of beef, it makes an ideal piece of stewing steak.

Place the beef flap fat down in a casserole on not too high a heat – this will render some of the fat, so that you have something to cook your onions in. Remove the beef, add the onions and cook until tender. It may seem an excessive amount of onion but they give off vital acid, which will help break the beef down into a hopefully tender beast.

Return the beef to the pan with the garlic, herbs, salt, pepper, wine and Trotter Gear, which will nurture the beef, as the onions will tenderise. Now cover with foil and place in a gentle oven. After 1½ hours, add the pickled walnuts. Cook for a further 2 hours, which gives you time for a bath and a couple of dry Martinis, sniffing the musk of your braised beef.

Cut into chunky slices and serve with mashed potato.

BRAISED SQUIRREL

1 squirrel per person, recipe to expand as you wish

PER SQUIRREL

a dollop of duck fat

5 shallots, peeled and left whole

4 dice-sized cubes of bacon

1 glass of Vieille Prune

a handful of dried porcini mushrooms, soaked in hot water for 2 hours, then drained

2 cloves of garlic, peeled and chopped

250g Trotter Gear (see page 42)

chicken stock (if needed)

½ bunch of watercress, trimmed

sea salt and black pepper

This is a dish that strikes me as a splendid use of squirrel, which is culled by gamekeepers all over the land in February, once the game season is over but their eye is still in. With flesh like oily wild rabbit, it cooks very well and tastes delicious.

A word of warning: you may have more luck tracking your squirrels down with a rural butcher. Ask for them skinned and jointed – 2 shoulders, 2 saddle sections and 2 hind legs.

Heat up the duck fat in a large casserole and brown the whole shallots. Add the squirrel and bacon and brown the meat. Flame in the pan using the Vieille Prune. Add the soaked porcini and garlic. Allow all to sizzle for a moment, then add the Trotter Gear and some salt and pepper. If it looks dry, add some chicken stock. Cover and braise in a gentle oven for 2½ hours. Check the thigh with a sharp knife – if yielding, remove the squirrel from the casserole and wilt the watercress in it, then bring the squirrel back into the pan. It's ready.

There is something quite poetic in the way the bosky wood the squirrel inhabits has been recreated – the earthy musk of the porcini and the watercress echoing the treetops.

SNAIL, TROTTER, SAUSAGE AND CHICKPEAS

To serve eight

400g dried chickpeas,
soaked in cold
water overnight

2 heads of garlic

12 shallots,
peeled and left whole

a splash of olive oil

some green bacon
chunks (you can never
fit in enough pork
with a pulse)

12 cloves of garlic,
peeled and left whole

500g Trotter Gear
(see page 42)

a bundle of thyme,
rosemary and
parsley stalks

10 small chorizo
sausages

40 fresh snails
(I refer you to Tony the
Snail Man on page 15)

2 bunches of rocket

Vinaigrette
(see page 210)

sea salt and black pepper

A steady *bowl* affair, this should bring comfort to many on a cold day.

Drain the chickpeas, cover with fresh water and add the heads of garlic. Bring to the boil, then cook at a gentle simmer for about 3 hours – you want totally submissive chickpeas or the giving nature of the dish will be lost.

Gently brown off the shallots in the oil, then add the green bacon. Allow to sizzle, then add the garlic cloves, Trotter Gear, bundle of herbs and whole chorizo. With a slotted spoon, add the chickpeas and any of the chickpea juice required – you are looking for a dampness.

Allow to simmer together for 20 minutes, then remove the chorizo and test the mixture for seasoning. Chop the chorizo into finger-width slices and return them to the chickpeas. Add the snails, stir and cover. Transfer to a medium-hot oven and bake for 35 minutes. When ready, chop the rocket in a disciplining fashion but don't crush it into submission. Dress it with vinaigrette and place on top of the snail/chickpea dish. The important thing to remember here is that this is a rocket top, not a garnish.

PIE POSSIBILITIES

To serve four with large appetites or six of a less gutsy disposition

a dollop of duck fat

a 450g piece of smoked bacon, skin off and kept, cut into cork-sized chunks

14 shallots, peeled but left whole

½ bottle of red wine

500g Trotter Gear (see page 42)

a spot of chicken stock up your sleeve

a 7–8cm piece of bone marrow

sea salt and black pepper

ANY ONE OF THE FOLLOWING:

5 pigeon

5 grouse

2 pheasant

1 hare

2 wild rabbit

This is one of Trotter Gear's finest moments, in a game pie. This recipe could be used for pigeon, rabbit, hare, pheasant or grouse pie. Rook is another story, which I will explain later. Your game should be on the bone; if rabbit or hare, it should be jointed.

Pie-making is rather like gathering our chums together under one suet crust.

Heat up the duck fat in a deep oven tray and brown off the game, bacon and shallots. Add the red wine and allow to simmer for a moment, then add the Trotter Gear. If the ingredients are not covered entirely, top up with chicken stock. Pop the bacon skin in. Cover the tray with foil and braise in a gentle oven for about 2 hours, until the game comes away from the bone with ease. When satisfied that this is the case, allow the mixture to cool and pull the flesh off the bones. Discard the bones and tear the game meat into pie-sized pieces. This is a matter of personal taste. Return the meat to the mixture and check the seasoning.

Leave this mixture to sit overnight in the fridge, allowing it to come to terms with its new role in life, and improve in flavour.

SUET PASTRY

250g self-raising flour

125g minced fresh beef suet

a pinch of salt

125–150ml water

1 egg, lightly beaten, to glaze

Next day find an appropriate pie dish and fill with the mixture, but not till it is falling over the edge. Nustle your piece of bone marrow into the middle of the dish so it is standing upright.

For the suet pastry, place the flour, suet and salt in a large bowl and mix together until the suet starts to break down. Then mix in enough water to make a firm paste. Wrap in cling film and leave to rest in the fridge for a few hours.

Roll out the pastry 6mm thick and use to cover the pie, moistening the rim of the dish first. Cut a hole for the bone marrow to stick through, slice off excess pastry from the sides, then press the edge down on to the moistened rim. Paint the top with the whisked-up egg.

It is ready for the oven, a hot oven, where it will need about 35–40 minutes. Watch that the pastry does not burn; reduce the oven temperature if it starts to look too dark. There is a tempting singe and there is burnt – very different!

Let us not forget the rook. In this case bring together your pie filling as before but without the game element, until the construction of the pie, when you should slip in the raw breasts of 6 rooks; otherwise stay true to the course set before.

TWO PIES

CHICKEN AND OX TONGUE PIE

To serve 4

1 ox tongue, brined for 10–14 days (see page 208)

stock vegetables – an onion, carrot and bundle of herbs

1 happy chicken, poached with onion, leek, peppercorns and garlic at a gentle simmer for 45 minutes (keep the stock)

2 onions, peeled and sliced

2 large knobs of butter

a handful of plain flour

1.2 litres milk

a big handful of extra-fine capers

½ quantity of Puff Pastry (see page 60)

1 egg, lightly beaten

sea salt and black pepper

For those of us who sometimes feel a little frail, here is a pie that will sort you out for sure.

Rinse the brined ox tongue and soak it for a couple of hours in fresh water. Poach it very gently for 3 hours with the onion, carrot and bundle of herbs – check it's thoroughly giving. Peel while still warm and cut in half. Use one half for sandwiches and the other for this pie.

Remove the chicken from the bone and cut it into pie-sized chunks. Slice the tongue about 5mm thick, so you will have a chunky chickeny, tonguey weave going on.

Cook the sliced onions in a knob of butter until totally submissive, then mix with the chicken and tongue and place in a pie dish.

Now make your white sauce. Melt the second knob of butter in a pan, add the flour and stir. Do not let it burn or colour but when it smells biscuity, start to add the milk. A whisk is a good thing at this moment. As it thickens, add more milk and whisk again. Hopefully we should end up with about a litre of creamy white sauce, which we let down with a little of the chicken stock and simmer until the word *silky* comes to mind.

Drain the capers and add to the sauce. Check the sauce for seasoning and pour it over the combination mixture in the pie dish.

Roll out the puff pastry to 7mm thick and use to cover the pie. Brush with the beaten egg and make a small hole in the centre of the pastry. Bake in a hot oven for 30–40 minutes, until well browned.

There we go, frail no longer.

PIKE PIE

The size of your pike might influence your pie size

1 pike

8 leeks, sliced length-
ways in half, then cut
across at 1cm intervals

2 large knobs of butter

a handful of plain flour

1–2 glasses of white wine

½ quantity of
Puff Pastry
(see page 60)

1 egg, lightly beaten

sea salt and black pepper

COURT-BOUILLON

a healthy splash of
white wine

a splash of vinegar

2 carrots, chopped

2 celery stalks, chopped

1 onion,
peeled and chopped

I always believed there was a huge pike living in Hampstead Ponds that would pull you under and, once you had stopped struggling, would feast upon you. Not a great introduction to pike, mythical or not, but I'm glad to say my pike awareness has come on in leaps and bounds, culminating in Pike Pie.

Find a pan large enough to hold your pike and fill it with water. Add all the court-bouillon ingredients and bring to a simmer. Add the pike and poach gently until it comes easily from the bones. Remove the pike from the court-bouillon, which is now delicious fish stock. Remove the bones and skin from the flesh.

Sweat the chopped leeks in a knob of butter until soft, then mix with the pike flesh and use to fill an appropriate-sized pie dish. You are looking for a good showing of leeks.

Now, follow the previous recipe's advice on white sauce except, once the flour and butter mixture smells biscuity, add the white wine instead of milk. From there on in, add our delicious fish stock until *silky* springs to mind again. Check for seasoning and pour this sauce over the pike and leeks.

1 *clove of garlic,*
peeled and chopped

a few peppercorns

a bay leaf

a few parsley stalks

Roll out the puff pastry and use to cover the pie. Brush with the beaten egg and make a small hole in the centre of the pastry. Bake in a hot oven for 30–40 minutes, until well browned.

A magnificent pie.

PUFF PASTRY

500g strong white flour

2 tsp sea salt

125g cold unsalted butter, diced, plus 375g cold unsalted butter

225ml cold water

2 tsp white wine vinegar

Sift the flour into a bowl, then add the salt and the 125g diced butter. Rub the butter in with your fingertips until the mixture looks like breadcrumbs. Then add the water and vinegar and mix together until you have a firm paste. Shape into a ball, wrap in cling film and leave in the fridge overnight.

The next day, take the pastry out of the fridge and leave it to soften for 1–2 hours. The remaining butter should be at the same temperature as the pastry (this is very important, as if the butter is too soft it will melt and ooze out of the pastry, whereas if it is too hard it will break though the pastry and ruin your puff). A good way to achieve the correct temperature is to put the butter between a couple of sheets of baking parchment (or re-use your butter wrappers) and beat it with a rolling pin to soften it.

When the butter and pastry are at the correct temperature, you are ready to roll out your pastry. First roll the pastry into a square, then roll out each side in turn to extend the square into a cross. Leave the centre thick, and be careful to keep the ends and sides square. Place the softened butter in the centre of the pastry, moulding it to the right size if necessary, so it fits neatly. Then wrap the arms of your cross over and around the butter – start by putting the left arm over the butter, then the right arm over the first arm, next the top and finally the bottom arm. The four arms of your cross should add up to the same thickness as the centre of the pastry. Now you have butter in a pastry package.

Turn your pastry so the top seam is on the right-hand side and roll it out on a floured surface into a rectangle about 20cm wide and 70cm long. Brush the excess flour off, then fold the rectangle in three, like a letter, with one end of the rectangle to the centre and the other end over this. Give the pastry a quarter turn, so the seam is on the right-hand side, then roll out and fold again. Wrap in cling film and leave to rest in the fridge for about 4 hours. Repeat twice more, so you have rolled out the pastry and butter six times, resting it after every two turns. Finally, wrap it in cling film and store in the fridge until ready to use. It also keeps well in the freezer.

MISCELLANEOUS DISHES WITHOUT TROTTER GEAR

DEEP-FRIED TRIPE

To serve four

*a bowl of plain flour
(about 250g)*

*a healthy pinch of
cayenne pepper*

*a deep-fat fryer or
large saucepan full of
clean vegetable oil*

*800g cleaned and cooked
white honeycomb tripe,
cut into pieces not
dissimilar in size to a
prawn cracker*

*Pickled Onions
(see the recipe for Pickled
Shallots on page 212)
and their vinegar*

sea salt and black pepper

A celebration of the soothing powers of tripe, this time with a little crunch to it.

Season the flour with salt, pepper and cayenne for a little piquancy, but not enough to lose its soothing edge.

Heat the oil up in whatever cooking arrangement you have. When hot, toss the tripe in the seasoned flour, shake off excess in a sieve and slip it into the oil. Deep-fry in batches until golden. Rescue from the oil and tip on to kitchen paper to remove excess oil.

Serve immediately with pickled onion vinegar for dipping, and chips. Ahhh!

SPINACH, DIJON MUSTARD AND CRÈME FRAÎCHE

a big bag of spinach,
stalks removed, washed,
then cooked down
in butter

a healthy spoonful of
Dijon mustard

a handful of grated hard
sheep's milk cheese
or Parmesan

a dollop of crème fraîche

sea salt and black pepper

This is a splendid dollop of green with a difference. All you need is a Magimix to whizz the ingredients.

It is as easy as whizzing all the ingredients together, then eating. Do not refrigerate.

It has numerous companions, meat, fish or fowl, and everyone goes yum!

BRAISED SHOULDER OF LAMB

To serve four, possibly five

1 *shoulder of lamb,*
on the bone

20 *shallots, peeled*
and left whole

20 *cloves of garlic,*
peeled and left whole

a splash of olive oil

a bundle of thyme
and rosemary

½ *bottle of white wine*

1 *litre light chicken stock*

sea salt and black pepper

Chop, leg, best end of lamb are all splendid, but a slow-braised shoulder of lamb ... aahhh! A piece of meat with a truly giving nature.

In an oven tray deep and wide enough to house your shoulder of lamb, brown the shallots and garlic in oil. Lay the bundle of joy in the pan and put the shoulder of lamb on top. Pour on the white wine and stock. Season the shoulder liberally.

Cover with foil and place in a gentle oven for 3-ish hours, as always keeping an eye on it and poking it with a small, sharp knife to check if it's done. As far as cooking meat goes, shoulder of lamb is one of the best-behaved joints and you don't even have to know how to carve. It is a case of attack.

GRILLED MACKEREL

This recipe has quite particular requirements but, as with any of these recipes, please feel free to adapt them to suit your own situation.

A driftwood fire on a beach in the Hebrides, mackerel caught that day, filleted (put knife in behind the gills, turn towards its tail, following the backbone, pull the knife down towards the tail, then flip over and repeat on the other side). When the embers are just so, place the mackerel, skin-side down, on the griddle. By the time the skin is happy and crispy, the fillets should be cooked.

Pop into a bap with some horseradish, sit on a rock and eat with lots of white wine. 'Did anyone remember to pack the corkscrew?'

GREY MULLET, FENNEL TWIGS AND JERUSALEM ARTICHOKES

To serve two

800g Jerusalem artichokes, washed but not peeled

an 800g grey mullet, gutted and scaled

a handful of fennel twigs (you can dry these yourself, or some smart fish shops sell them)

a spot of olive oil

a big knob of butter

2 lemon halves

sea salt and black pepper

There seems an earthy synergy between this fish and the Jerusalem artichoke and, as far as I know, the grey mullet is still plentiful in these days of diminishing fish stocks.

Boil the Jerusalem artichokes in salty water until tender, then drain.

Season the fish liberally inside and out and nustle the fennel twigs into its cavity. Get an ovenproof frying pan (large enough to hold your fish) very hot. Add the oil and butter and allow a little sizzle. Slip your fish in. Wiggle the pan for a moment, so the fish does not stick, then surround it with the boiled Jerusalem artichokes. Roll these around in the butter and pop the pan into a hot oven.

After about 7 minutes, when the fish has turned a convincing colour, turn it over and cook for another 7 minutes. It should be just about there and the artichokes should take on a nutty quality. Serve up with the lemon.

COLD ROAST BEEF ON DRIPPING TOAST

Another of those treats for the day after, having saved the dripping from the previous day's roast.

Spread dripping on to a slice of white toast and put under the grill for a moment to make sure it melts completely. Sprinkle with coarse sea salt and pop a thin slice of yesterday's cold beef on top. Open a jar of pickled walnuts. A glass of something Burgundian. Life is good!

VENISON LIVER

Venison offal is a joy. For some reason I imagined it would taste dark, bitter and of iron – how wrong could I have been? Venison liver is sweet, delicate and tender. I have heard that their brains are fantastic, but are the culinary treat of the gillie.

A plea: use venison offal when you can, treat as other offal, just make sure you know for your own peace of mind where it harks from.

Venison liver goes very well with roasted beetroot, mash or braised chicory.

MINCE AND TATTIES

To serve six

1 onion, peeled and
thinly sliced

1 leek, cleaned, sliced
lengthways in half, then
thinly sliced across

1 carrot, peeled, sliced
lengthways in half, then
thinly sliced across

4 cloves of garlic,
peeled and chopped

a splash of olive oil

1kg minced beef

2 tinned tomatoes

a handful of oatmeal

1 shot glass of
Worcestershire sauce

⅓ bottle of red wine, my
gesture to the
old alliance

chicken stock, if needed

a dozen proper
boiling potatoes

sea salt and black pepper

A dish discussed as much as cassoulet is in Castelnaudary. Questions such as should you add peas or carrots can start a gastronomic row of great proportions. Sticking my neck out, I know Caledonia MacBrayne adds peas to its mince but I don't, although I do like a spot of carrot in mine. It gets worse – I can't help making a small gesture to the old alliance as well. If you haven't tossed this book away in disgust already, here are my mince thoughts.

In a large pan, sweat the onion, leek, carrot and garlic in the splash of olive oil until softened. Add the mince, giving it a healthy stir to break it up. Add the tinned tomatoes, crushed in your hand – a subliminal gesture. Keep stirring and add the oatmeal, not so much that you end up with a porridge. Stir, add the Worcestershire sauce and red wine, then stir again. Take a view on the liquid content; if it seems a wee bit dry, add some stock. You are looking for a loose lava consistency. Check for seasoning.

Now allow the mince to simmer gently for 1½ hours, if not 2 (if it is drying out, add more stock). Time allows the mince to become itself, as is the case for most of us.

While the mince cooks, peel the potatoes and simply boil them in salty water. After a long journey, there is no dish more welcoming. Also, a dram doesn't go amiss.

ROAST WHOLE SUCKLING PIG

1 appropriately
sized piglet

olive oil

sea salt and black pepper

STUFFING

4 red onions, peeled
and sliced

a dollop of duck fat

½ bottle of red wine

the kidneys
from the pig, chopped

about ½ loaf of
yesterday's white bread

2 cloves of garlic,
peeled and crushed

8 sage leaves, chopped

It's very important to keep in mind the size of your oven when purchasing your suckling pig. There is nothing sadder than a wee pig ready to roast and it won't fit in the oven. So ...

Cook the red onions in the duck fat until completely tender. Pour in the red wine. Let this simmer and reduce until you have a *moving* marmalade of red onion. Add the chopped-up kidneys from the piglet and some chunks of yesterday's white bread. Season and stir. At this point you should have a mass of bread cubes held together by an onion weave. Take off the heat and add the garlic and sage to the mix.

Now stuff your piglet, rather like those cuddly animals you kept your pyjamas in. The stuffing will swell, being designed to be receptive of all the piggy juices, so some rudimentary sewing up of the pig is required.

Sit the pig on an oven tray in a sphinx-like manner, then rub some oil on to it as if it is Ambre Solaire on a good friend's back. Season liberally and place in a medium oven for 3 to 4 hours. You want a pig at the end that offers no resistance to your carving. Gather friends and have a feast.

ORBS OF JOY

This might sound peculiar but does make the perfect accompaniment to a grey-legged partridge. One Orb of Joy per person.

Peel some red onions but keep them whole. Put in an oven dish and add chicken stock until they are almost covered. Braise them in a medium oven. As they cook, the stock around them will reduce slightly, giving your onions a slightly singed and caramelized exterior and a pale pink and totally giving interior. Truly an orb of joy!

WHAT A BAKED POTATO

To serve four

4 large jacket potatoes

*20 cloves of garlic,
peeled and left whole*

*enough duck fat to
cover the garlic*

sea salt and black pepper

We seem to have moved into the realms of comfort food, and they don't come more comforting than these hot potatoes.

Bake the potatoes in a medium oven until soft to the squeeze. Meanwhile, put the garlic cloves into an ovenproof dish and cover with the duck fat. Cover the dish and put into a gentle to medium oven. Cook until the garlic is totally squishy, then remove from the oven and whizz the garlic and enough of the duck fat in a food processor to give a very loose paste.

Let the potatoes cool enough to handle, then cut them in half lengthways. Scoop out the flesh into a bowl and add the garlic and duck fat paste. Stir thoroughly. When they have combined forces, season and return to the hollow potato skins. Pop into a hot oven until golden brown. Have you ever heard of *such* comforting fare?

CHEESY MOMENTS

WIGMORE AND POTATO PIE

To serve two

4 *potatoes,*
boiled and peeled

1 *ripe Wigmore cheese*

1 *egg, lightly beaten*

sea salt and black pepper

DOUGH

420g *plain flour, sifted*

2 *eggs*

1 *egg yolk*

100g *warm*
melted butter

a pinch of salt

100ml *warm water*

When you turn the pie out of the tin it resembles a cottage with subsidence. Word of warning: you want everyone at the table before you put your knife into the pie.

Don't let the dough go cold or it will be very difficult to use. The quantity given below makes enough for two goes, just in case.

To make the dough, place the flour, eggs, egg yolk, melted butter and salt in the bowl of an electric mixer. Using the beater attachment, mix the ingredients to a firm paste. Add the water and mix again until a soft, glossy, pliable dough is formed. Cover the bowl with a cloth and leave in a warm place for 30 minutes.

While the dough is resting, cut the potatoes into slices 1cm thick and do the same with the Wigmore cheese. Grease a 16 x 10 x 8cm loaf tin with butter and then dust it with flour.

Roll out half the pastry very thinly – about 3mm thick. Try to do this quite quickly so it doesn't go cold. Use the rolled-out dough to line the loaf tin, making sure you have about 2cm overhanging; trim off the rest. Cover the base of the pastry with some of the sliced potatoes – you will have to trim them a little – then season with salt and pepper. Add a layer of Wigmore cheese. Carry on layering until you reach the top of the tin, ending with a layer of potatoes.

Roll out a lid for the pie from the dough trimmings. Place the lid on top of the potatoes, then brush the overhanging dough with the beaten egg and fold it over the pastry lid to seal. Brush the top with more egg.

Place in an oven preheated to 180°C/Gas Mark 4 and bake for about 1 hour, until golden brown on top and piping hot in the middle. Serve with pickled walnuts.

FENNEL AND BERKSWELL

Berkswell, for those of you who have not encountered it before, is a magnificent, firm sheep's milk cheese. It seems almost cheeky to be cooking with it, but the results are splendid.

In an ovenproof dish, layer up fennel, sliced against the grain, and grated Berkswell, ending with a Berkswell layer. Season the dish, splash with milk so everything is more damp than wet, then cover and put into a gentle oven. Let it calmly do its thing.

After 2½ hours, take the lid off for a bit of colour. What you should end up with is a cake of sweet, collapsing fennel and curds and whey, like cheesy nuduals. As a dish, it has no end of companions, but will also stand alone with just a pickled walnut to keep it company.

I now pass you over to the very capable hands of Justin, to explore the world of Pastry, Pudding & Bread.

ORGANIC
OATE & SONS
ORGAN
AFTES
ANN MIL
LEPHONE (01747) 852
32 kgs
ORGA
ORGA

BREAD

MOTHER

1 stick of rhubarb

210ml water

2 tbsp live yoghurt

50g rye flour

50g wholemeal flour

100g strong white flour

The Mother forms the base of all our breads at St. John (except soda bread). We started ours about five years ago and have been looking after her ever since.

A Mother adds character to your bread. The flavour and texture of sourdough in particular come from using no commercial yeast, only your Mother. The process takes longer but the results are worth the wait.

DAY 1

Chop the rhubarb into slices 5mm thick and mix with the water and yoghurt. Add the flour and stir until you have a wet, lumpy mixture. Place in a clean container, dust with white flour and leave somewhere warm (around 26–28°C).

DAY 2

Just give the mixture a stir and dust with white flour again.

DAY 3

Stir it again; you should see signs of fermentation taking place. Add 4 tablespoons of white flour and 4 tablespoons of water, mix well and dust with white flour.

DAYS 4–5

On Day 4, discard about a third of the Mother and replace with a fresh quantity of all the ingredients except the rhubarb. Repeat on Day 5.

DAY 6

The Mother should now be ready to use in your bread making – it should be bubbly and smell strong and sour.

After making a loaf, you will need to replenish the Mother with half and half flour and water, in equal quantities to the amount you took out – so if you make the White Loaf (see page 92) for example, which uses 100g of the Mother, you would have to replace it with 50g flour and 50ml water. The type of flour you use for replenishment depends on which loaf you plan to make next: for a white loaf use strong white flour; for brown, use 25g strong white flour and 25g wholemeal flour.

After replenishing, leave the Mother to ferment for a day before use. You can leave it in the fridge without feeding for months but it will take a few days to restart it by feeding it – again, discard about a third and feed it equal parts flour and water. Repeat this until there are signs of fermentation.

WHITE LOAF

520g strong white flour

100g Mother
(see page 88)

340ml water (at 5°C)

½ tsp fresh yeast

60ml cold water
(known as the bathe)

10g sea salt

Bread is as vital as your knife and fork in the eating process.

MAKING THE DOUGH

Place the flour, Mother, water and yeast in an electric mixer and, using the dough hook attachment, mix on low speed for 6 minutes, making sure all the water is incorporated and the dough starts to leave the sides of the bowl clean. Leave to stand for 5 minutes, then start to pour in the bathe. We do this in three goes: add a third of the bathe to begin with and mix the dough for 4 minutes on a low speed. Add the next third of the bathe and mix for 4 minutes. Add the final third of the bathe and mix for 6 minutes, until the dough looks smooth. Leave it to rest for 10 minutes. Then add the salt and mix for 4 minutes, again until the dough looks smooth and leaves the sides of the bowl clean.

RISING

The dough will be quite wet. Roll it into a ball, return it to the mixing bowl and sprinkle with flour. Cover with a cloth, place in the fridge and leave for 1 hour.

Remove the dough from the fridge, shape it into a ball again, sprinkle with flour and cover. Leave it somewhere warm (about 20°C, or warm room temperature) for 3 hours, until slightly risen.

Take your dough and either shape it into one large ball or split it in half for two smaller loaves. Place on a floured baking tray, sprinkle with flour and cover. Leave to rest for 15 minutes.

SHAPING

We shape the loaf into a baton but you can choose your own shape and style. Try not to use too much flour when you are rolling, as it gets into the dough and you may be left with pockets of raw flour in your loaf. Once you have shaped it, place it on a baking sheet, sprinkle with flour and cover. Leave for 1–2 hours, until doubled in size.

BAKING

Preheat the oven to 230°C/Gas Mark 8. Place a heatproof bowl of water on the bottom of the oven. This will produce steam, which will form a better crust.

Remove the cloth from the bread and, using a razor blade or a very sharp knife (a razor blade is best), slash the top three times lengthways at an angle. Then place the loaf in the oven and bake for 30 minutes. Open the oven door to let out any excess steam, take out your bowl of water, then close the door and bake for a further 10 minutes. To test if the loaf is done, turn it over and tap it on the base with your finger; if it sounds hollow it is ready. Place on a wire rack to cool.

OLD DOUGH

1.25kg strong white flour

750ml water

5g fresh yeast

Like the Mother, above, Old Dough adds flavour and texture to a loaf.

Mix all the ingredients together, either by hand or in a machine, until well incorporated. Place in an oiled plastic container and leave in the fridge for 24 hours before use.

WHOLEMEAL LOAF

300g wholemeal flour

200g strong white flour

100g Mother
(see page 88)

340ml water (at 5°C)

½ tsp fresh yeast

75ml cold water
(known as the bathe)

10g sea salt

Make as for the White Loaf (see page 92) but take note: the dough will be firmer. We like to finish a wholemeal loaf by slashing a single cut along its length before baking.

WHITE SOURDOUGH LOAF

500g strong white flour

*130g Mother
(see page 88)*

320ml water (at 5°C)

*90ml cold water
(known as the bathe)*

10g sea salt

The offspring of Justin's much-nurtured Mother.

MAKING THE DOUGH

Place the flour, Mother and water in an electric mixer and, using the dough hook attachment, mix on low speed for 6 minutes, making sure all the water is incorporated and the dough starts to leave the sides of the bowl clean. Then start to pour in the bathe. Do this a third at a time, as we do for the White Loaf (see page 92). Leave the dough to rest for 20 minutes. Then add the salt and mix for 4 minutes, again until the dough looks smooth and leaves the sides of the bowl clean.

RISING

Shape the dough into a ball, then place it back in the mixing bowl and sprinkle with flour. Cover with a cloth, place in the fridge and leave for 1 hour.

Remove the dough from the fridge, shape it into a ball again, sprinkle with flour and cover. Then leave it somewhere warm (about 20°C, or warm room temperature) for about 3 hours, until slightly risen.

Take the dough and either shape it into one large ball or split it in half for two smaller loaves. Place on a floured tray, sprinkle with flour and cover. Leave to rest for 15 minutes.

SHAPING

We shape sourdough loaves into a ball but you can choose your own shape and style. Place the shaped loaf in a floured proving basket or a floured plastic bowl and sprinkle with flour. Cover with a cloth and leave for 4–5 hours, until doubled in size.

BAKING

Preheat the oven to 230°C/Gas Mark 8. Place a heatproof bowl of water on the bottom of the oven. This will produce steam, which will form a better crust.

Take the cloth off the bread and carefully transfer the loaf to a baking sheet. Using a razor blade or a very sharp knife (a razor blade is best), slash a cut round the circumference of the loaf in a single movement. Then place it in the oven and bake for 30 minutes. Open the oven door to let out any excess steam and take out the bowl of water. Close the door and bake for a further 10 minutes. To test if the loaf is done, turn it over and tap it on the base with your finger; if it sounds hollow it is ready. Place on a wire rack to cool.

BROWN SOURDOUGH LOAF

400g strong white flour

45g wholemeal flour

45g rye flour

*140g Mother
(see page 88)*

320ml water (at 5°C)

*80ml cold water
(known as the bathe)*

10g sea salt

Make as for the White Sourdough Loaf (see page 96). For a Brown Sourdough Loaf, we finish it before baking by slashing four cuts on top, about 7cm long, to form a square.

RAISIN LOAF

110g raisins

110g currants

400g strong white flour

75g Mother (see page 88)

½ tsp fresh yeast

30g unsalted butter

220ml water (at 5°C)

8g sea salt

Fantastic with goat's or sheep's milk cheese. Both these cheeses have the amazing ability to make your last glass of wine taste as good as the first.

Soak the raisins and currants overnight in enough warm water just to cover.

MAKING THE DOUGH

Strain the raisins and currants, keeping the liquid. Place the flour, Mother, yeast and butter in an electric mixer and, using the dough hook attachment, mix on medium speed for 2 minutes just to break down the butter. Then add the water and mix on low speed for 4 minutes.

Use the soaking liquid from the dried fruit as the bathe; you will need 100ml, so top up with a little more water if necessary. Add a third of the bathe to begin with and mix the dough for 5 minutes on low speed. Add the next third and mix for 5 minutes. Add the final third and mix for 6 minutes. Leave the dough to rest for 20 minutes, then add the salt, currants and raisins and mix for a further 5 minutes.

RISING

Your dough will be very wet and hard to handle, so good luck, and remember – try not to add too much flour. Roll the dough into a ball, return it to the mixing bowl and sprinkle with flour. Cover with a cloth, place in the fridge and leave for 1 hour.

Remove the dough from the fridge and shape it into a ball again. Sprinkle with flour, cover and leave it somewhere warm (about 20°C, or warm room temperature) for about 3 hours, until it has risen a little.

Take the dough and either shape it into one large ball or split it in half to make two smaller loaves. Place on a baking tray and leave to rest for 15 minutes.

SHAPING

Shape the dough into a baton as best you can and place in a buttered large loaf tin. Sprinkle with flour, cover and leave for 2 hours or until the dough reaches the top of the tin.

BAKING

Preheat the oven to 210°C/Gas Mark 6½. Place a heat-proof bowl of water on the bottom of the oven. This will produce steam, which will form a better crust.

Place the loaf in the oven and bake for 20 minutes. Open the oven door to let out any excess steam and remove the bowl of water. Carefully take the loaf out of the tin, lay it on its side on the oven shelf and bake for 5 minutes. Repeat on the other side, then remove from the oven and leave to cool on a wire rack.

SANDWICH LOAF

550g strong white flour

500g Old Dough
(see page 94)

30g fresh yeast

15g sea salt

275ml water

This is not white sliced pap; this is a handsome, white, crusty beauty, which speaks bacon sandwich.

Place all the ingredients in an electric mixer and, using the dough hook attachment, mix on medium speed for 6–8 minutes. Cover the dough and leave to prove in the bowl for just 10 minutes. Then divide into 5 balls and place them in a buttered large loaf tin. Dust with flour and cover loosely with a cloth. Leave in a warm place for 1 hour, until doubled in size.

Place in an oven preheated to 220°C/Gas Mark 7 and bake for 20 minutes, then carefully remove the loaf from the tin, lay it on its side on the oven shelf and bake for a further 8 minutes. Repeat on the other side, then remove the loaf from the oven and leave to cool on a wire rack.

SODA BREAD

140g wholemeal
self-raising flour

140g strong white flour

5g sea salt

10g caster sugar

5g baking powder

125ml water

125ml buttermilk

Fantastic toasted for breakfast with butter and Marmite.

Mix all the ingredients together by hand in a large mixing bowl (it will be quite wet), then leave the dough to rest in the bowl for 5 minutes.

Shape the dough into a ball and place on a floured baking tray. Sprinkle with flour and cut a cross in the top about 4cm long on each side and 1cm deep. Leave to rest for 10 minutes, then place in an oven preheated to 200°C/Gas Mark 6. Bake for 40 minutes, until golden brown. To test if the loaf is done, turn it over and tap it on the bottom with your finger; if it sounds hollow it is ready. Leave to cool on a wire rack. Serve with plenty of butter.

BAKING AND DOUGHNUTS

SEED CAKE AND A GLASS
OF MADEIRA

*260g softened
unsalted butter*

260g caster sugar

1 tsp caraway seeds

*5 large eggs,
lightly beaten*

320g self-raising flour

150ml full-fat milk

**Eleven o'clock and still two hours until lunchtime.
Something to keep you steady – nothing finer than
a slice of seed cake, washed down by a glass of
Madeira. This will see you safely through until
lunch.**

Grease a 16 x 10 x 8cm loaf tin with butter and
line the base and sides with baking parchment.

Cream the butter, sugar and caraways together
either with an electric mixer or in a bowl with a
wooden spoon until they are white and fluffy.
Gradually mix in the beaten eggs, adding them
little by little to prevent curdling. Then sift in the
flour and mix until incorporated. Lastly add the
milk.

Transfer the mixture to the prepared tin and bake
in an oven preheated to 180°C/Gas Mark 4 for
45 minutes or until it is golden brown and a skewer
inserted in the centre comes out clean.

Serve with a glass of Madeira.

LITTLE CHOCOLATE BUNS

Makes a dozen

210g strong white flour

90g Old Dough
(see page 94)

35ml olive oil

5g fresh yeast

55ml full-fat milk

1 tsp salt

65ml water

12 squares of dark
chocolate, with at least
70 per cent cocoa solids

cocoa powder
for dusting

There is nothing finer than warm little buttock-like buns.

Place the flour, dough, oil, yeast, milk, salt and water in the bowl of an electric mixer and, with the dough hook, mix for around 6–8 minutes, until smooth and elastic. Cover the dough and leave to prove for just 10 minutes. Then divide it into 12 balls and flatten out each one. Place a square of chocolate in the middle of the dough and pull the dough around it so it is completely enclosed. Reshape the dough into a ball and place on a floured baking tray. The buns will spread, so be sure to allow a little room between each one. Dust with cocoa powder, cover loosely with cling film and prove in a warm place for 2 hours.

Bake in an oven preheated to 200°C/Gas Mark 6 for 15 minutes, until the buns are golden brown. Serve immediately from the oven. Watch out, the filling will be like molten lava. Blow blow.

LITTLE PRUNE BUNS

Makes a dozen

Make these as for the chocolate version (see page 109), replacing the chocolate with 12 prunes and brushing the tops with beaten egg rather than dusting them with cocoa powder.

LITTLE ANCHOVY BUNS

Makes a dozen

ingredients as for Little Chocolate Buns (page 109), minus the chocolate and cocoa powder

ANCHOVY PASTE

7 garlic cloves, peeled

a pinch of black pepper

1 tin of anchovies in oil, drained

up to 285ml extra virgin olive oil

a splash of red wine vinegar

In Florence there is a fantastic place with a wee slip of a bar, which offers little buns and a glass of white wine, just for those moments when you need some sustenance to keep you going in the day. Here is our take on the little steadying bun.

To make the anchovy paste, crush the garlic and pepper to a fine purée in a food processor or with a pestle and mortar, then add the anchovies and allow them to break down. Gradually add just enough oil to make a thick paste, then the vinegar to taste. Check the seasoning.

Make and shape the dough as for the chocolate buns, but without a filling. After baking, let them cool slightly, then slice them in half. Spread with the paste and sandwich them back together.

The anchovy paste can have many uses, depending on how thick you make it. With less oil and vinegar added, you will have a very firm paste, which is delicious spread on toast and eaten with sweet roasted shallots. If the full amount of oil is added, you will have a looser, though still emulsified, mixture, which is ideal for dressing boiled greens or broccoli – eat them on their own or with lamb or beef. It also makes an excellent dressing for bitter salad leaves.

PRUNE LOAF

125g softened
unsalted butter

110g soft light
brown sugar

3 large eggs,
lightly beaten

225g plain flour

1 tsp bicarbonate of soda

2 tbsp vanilla extract

4 tbsp black treacle

3 tbsp prune juice

3 tbsp full-fat milk

600g tea-soaked prunes
(see page 134)

MIST

75ml prune juice

25ml Vieille Prune

Onomatopoeically a joy.

Grease a 30 x 11 x 7cm loaf tin with butter and line the base and sides with baking parchment.

Cream the butter and sugar together either with an electric mixer or in a bowl with a wooden spoon until they are white and fluffy. Gradually beat in the eggs, adding them little by little to prevent curdling. Sift in the flour and bicarbonate of soda and mix in. Then add the vanilla extract, black treacle, prune juice and milk. This should leave you with a fairly wet mixture.

Fill the lined loaf tin just over half way with the mixture. Place the prunes on top, patting them down gently, but not all the way to the bottom, so they're evenly distributed. Chill in the fridge for 2 hours. This stops the prunes sinking to the bottom of the loaf.

Bake in an oven preheated to 180°C/Gas Mark 4 for 45–50 minutes, until a skewer inserted into the middle of the loaf comes out clean. Remove from the oven, place on a cooling rack and leave for 10 minutes before serving.

Now for the mist: heat the prune juice in a small saucepan until it starts to boil, then add the Vieille Prune and take it off the heat. Serve the loaf warm, with extra-thick Jersey cream or vanilla ice cream, and pour 2 tablespoons of mist over each serving.

TRENCHER

Big enough for a large joint

110ml full-fat milk

60ml water

5g fresh yeast

275g strong white flour

5g caster sugar

5g salt

40g beef dripping

No finer thing than roast beef oozing into a trencher.

Heat the milk and water to blood temperature (37.5°C), then remove from the heat. Add the yeast and mix until dissolved. Leave in a warm place for about 10 minutes.

Sift the flour, sugar and salt into a bowl and rub in half the dripping. Add the yeast mixture and stir well to form a dough. Cover with a cloth and leave in a warm place for 10–15 minutes. Remove the dough from the bowl and knead on a floured work surface for 5 minutes, until smooth and elastic. Cover again and leave in a warm place for 25 minutes, until doubled in size.

Roll out the dough so it is a good 2–3cm bigger all round than your joint of meat. Place on a baking tray, cover and leave to prove for about 25 minutes, until doubled in size again. Bake in an oven preheated to 200°C/Gas Mark 6 for 20 minutes, until golden brown.

Slice the top off the trencher (just a thin slice) and discard it. Dot the rest of the dripping over the trencher and put it in the oven for just a few moments to melt. Place on a serving dish, pour some gravy over it and put the joint of meat on top. Then give the meat its normal resting time, so all the lovely juices get sucked into the trencher.

MADELEINES

Makes about two dozen

135g *unsalted butter*

2 tbsp *pure honey*

3 *large eggs*

110g *caster sugar*

15g *soft light brown sugar*

135g *self-raising flour, sifted*

Well, I feel Proust must have covered most aspects but what about a plate of warm madeleines in the afternoon with a bottle of pink Champagne? Almost as good as elevenses.

You will need a madeleine tray.

Melt the butter and honey in a saucepan and simmer until golden brown. Leave to cool. Using an electric mixer, whisk the eggs, caster sugar and brown sugar together for 8–10 minutes, until the mixture has tripled in volume and leaves a trail on the surface for a few seconds when the whisk is lifted.

Fold the sifted flour and melted butter though the egg mixture until it is all incorporated. Pour into a plastic container and leave to rest in the fridge for 2–3 hours.

Grease the madeleine moulds with butter, then dust them with flour, tapping off any excess. Place a dessertspoon of the mixture in each mould and bake in an oven preheated to 190°C/Gas Mark 5 for 12–15 minutes, until firm to the touch and golden brown.

SHORTBREAD

Makes twenty to thirty biscuits, enough to fill your biscuit tin right to the top

750g plain flour

500g cold unsalted butter, cut into small cubes

250g caster sugar

Shortbread is rather like Lutyens' Castle Drogo, which he built with three ingredients: wood, glass and stone. Both are splendid.

Sift the flour into a large bowl, add the butter and rub them together with your fingertips. What you are looking for is a breadcrumb consistency; when you reach that stage, add the sugar and rub it in until you have a smooth paste. It will be a little crumbly but that comes from the shortness of the mix. Wrap the dough in cling film and let it rest in the fridge for about 30 minutes.

Roll out on a lightly floured surface to about 8mm thick and then cut into rounds with a 3cm pastry cutter. Place on baking trays lined with baking parchment and bake in an oven preheated to 160°C/Gas Mark 3 for about 10–15 minutes. The shortbread should be very pale, so be careful not to overcook it.

THINS

Makes lots; but the raw dough keeps very well in the freezer

450g unsalted butter

450g caster sugar, plus extra for sprinkling

2 large eggs

580g plain flour, sifted

a pinch of salt

2 tsp baking powder

1 tsp vanilla extract

ONE OF THE FOLLOWING FLAVOURINGS:

3–4 tsp ground cinnamon or ginger

2–3 tsp grated orange or lemon zest

1–2 tsp liquid malt

It's strange how the word *thins* onomatopoeically gets one going.

Cream the butter and sugar together until light and fluffy, then beat in the eggs one at a time. Beat in the sifted flour, salt, baking powder, vanilla extract and your chosen flavouring. Shape the dough into a log about 20 x 2 x 8cm, wrap in cling film and chill for about 30 minutes, until firm.

Slice the log as thinly as you can (that's why they are Thins, not Thicks) and place on a baking sheet lined with baking parchment (you can just slice off as many as you need, then wrap the remaining dough and keep it in the fridge or freezer). Bake in an oven preheated to 160°C/Gas Mark 3 for 5–8 minutes, until golden brown. Remove from the oven, sprinkle with caster sugar and leave to cool.

HAZELNUT BISCUITS

Makes lots

140g *unsalted butter*

140g *caster sugar*

1 *large egg yolk*

140g *plain flour*

280g *whole
roasted hazelnuts*

Perfect to serve with Bitter Chocolate Cream (see page 142).

Using an electric mixer, cream the butter and sugar together until white and fluffy, then beat in the egg yolk. Mix in the flour, followed by the roasted hazelnuts. Mix on full speed for 2–4 minutes to break down the hazelnuts a little. Remove the dough from the mixing bowl and roll it into a log about 3cm in diameter. Wrap in cling film and chill for 1–2 hours.

Cut the log into slices 5mm thick and place on a baking sheet lined with baking parchment. The biscuits will spread, so be sure to leave a little room between each one. Bake in an oven preheated to 160°C/Gas Mark 3 for 10 minutes or until golden.

SPECULAAS

Makes fifteen to twenty

125g unsalted butter

150g Demerara sugar

grated zest of 1 lemon

250g plain flour

½ tsp baking powder

a pinch of salt

30g flaked almonds

10g mixed candied peel, finely chopped

100ml full-fat milk

SPICE MIX

2 tbsp ground cinnamon

2 tsp ground nutmeg

2 tsp ground cloves

2 tsp ground mace

2 tsp ground ginger

Great name, great biscuit.

Mix together all the ingredients for the spice mix (you won't need it all for this recipe but it will keep well in a tightly sealed jar).

Cream the butter, sugar and lemon zest together for 3–4 minutes. The mixture will not go light and fluffy because of the coarse grains of the sugar but creaming it will bring out the flavour of the lemon. Sift in the flour, baking powder, salt and 3 teaspoons of the spice mix and fold them in. It won't form a dough because the liquid has not been added yet. Now stir in the flaked almonds and mixed peel. Lastly stir in the milk to form a dough. Shape it into a log about 3cm thick, wrap in cling film and chill for 1–2 hours.

Cut the dough into slices about 4mm thick and place them on a baking tray lined with baking parchment. The biscuits will spread, so leave a little room between each one. Bake in an oven preheated to 160°C/Gas Mark 3 for 10–15 minutes, until golden brown.

ECCLES CAKES

It's good to put things right.

Since the first book, *Nose to Tail Eating*, I have changed the way we assemble the Eccles cake. Rather than sandwiching two discs of puff pastry together, we now use a single disc approximately 9cm in diameter. So place your Eccles cake mix in the centre of the disc and pull up the sides of the pastry to cover the filling. Seal it with your fingers, then turn it over and slash the top.

The reason we slash the top of the Eccles cake three times is for the Holy Trinity (well, that's what I have been told).

DOUGHNUTS

Makes twenty-five

500g strong white flour

65g caster sugar, plus
extra for coating

10g salt

15g fresh yeast

4 large eggs

grated zest of 1 lemon

155ml water

125g softened
unsalted butter

sunflower oil
for deep-frying

I've tried eating Justin's doughnuts without licking my lips. I was doing well, then the custard spurted on to my glasses – that was the moment when loss of concentration led to lip licking.

A weakness for custard aside, all Justin's dough-nuts have the *licko lip* factor.

You will need a freestanding electric mixer fitted with the beater attachment.

Place all the ingredients except the butter and oil in the bowl of the mixer. Mix on medium speed for 6 minutes, then scrape down the sides of the bowl. Start mixing on medium speed again, adding the soft butter about 20g at a time until all incorporated. Keep mixing for 6–8 minutes, until the dough has come away from the sides of the bowl and looks smooth, glossy and elastic.

Place the dough in a large bowl, sprinkle the surface with flour and cover the bowl with a tea towel. Leave to rise for 2–3 hours in a warm place, until doubled in size, then knock back the dough. Cover the bowl with cling film and place in the fridge for at least 4 hours or overnight.

Cut the dough into 25 pieces and roll them into smooth balls. Place on floured baking sheets, leaving about 5cm between each one. Cover with cling film and leave to prove for 2–3 hours, depending on how warm it is; they should double in size.

Half-fill a deep-fat fryer or a deep, heavy-based saucepan with sunflower oil and heat it to 190°C. The temperature is very important: too high and the doughnuts will burn; too low and they will absorb the oil, making them greasy.

With the oil at the right temperature, start frying the doughnuts, in batches of 3 or 4 at a time, until golden brown. They will take about 2 minutes on each side. Remember to check the temperature of the oil between each batch. As the doughnuts are done, place them on kitchen paper to soak up excess oil and then toss in caster sugar.

The doughnuts are fantastic on their own but on Sundays we sell them at the bakery at St. John Bread & Wine filled with crème pâtissière, lemon curd, chocolate custard, apple and cinnamon and homemade jam. So the next five recipes are for doughnut fillings and their possibilities.

If you decide to fill your doughnuts, you will need a piping bag with a nozzle. Make a hole in each doughnut with a small knife and pipe in the filling. We fill them very generously – about 4 tablespoons of filling per doughnut.

CRÈME PÂTISSIÈRE

Makes enough to fill twenty-five doughnuts

2 vanilla pods

1 litre full-fat milk

12 large egg yolks

130g caster sugar

80g plain flour

250ml lightly whipped double cream (optional)

Slit the vanilla pods lengthways and scrape out the seeds. Put the pods and seeds in a saucepan with the milk and bring to the boil over a medium heat.

Meanwhile, mix the egg yolks and sugar together in a large bowl. Sift in the flour and whisk all together. When the milk is boiling, pour it over the egg mixture, whisking all the time. Then return the mixture to the saucepan and slowly bring to the boil over a low heat, whisking occasionally. Once it is boiling, whisk continuously for about 5 minutes, until very thick and smooth. Strain through a fine sieve into a bowl and cover the surface with cling film to prevent a skin forming. Leave to cool, then chill. (Keep the vanilla pods; if you wash them out, dry them in a low oven and store in a jar of caster sugar. You will have some lovely vanilla sugar in a month or two.)

If using the crème pâtissière for doughnuts, lighten it up by folding the whipped cream into it.

CRÈME PÂTISSIÈRE: ITS POSSIBILITIES

Custard slice
Tarts
Pancakes
Mousses
Profiteroles

CHOCOLATE CUSTARD

Makes enough to fill twenty-five doughnuts

1 litre full-fat milk

12 large egg yolks

130g caster sugar

65g plain flour

200g plain chocolate, with at least 70 per cent cocoa solids, finely chopped

250ml lightly whipped double cream (optional)

Pour the milk into a saucepan and bring to the boil over a medium heat. Meanwhile, mix the egg yolks and sugar together in a large bowl. Sift in the flour and whisk all together. When the milk is boiling, pour it over the egg mixture, whisking all the time. Then return the mixture to the saucepan and slowly bring to the boil over a low heat, whisking occasionally.

Once it is boiling, whisk continuously for about 5 minutes, until very thick and smooth. Strain through a fine sieve into a heatproof bowl. Add the chocolate and whisk it into the hot custard until dissolved. Cover the surface with cling film to prevent a skin forming, leave to cool, then chill.

If using the chocolate custard for doughnuts, we like to lighten it up by folding the whipped cream into it.

CHOCOLATE CUSTARD: ITS POSSIBILITIES

Black forest trifle
Pancakes
Tarts
Profiteroles
Chocolate cake
Custard slice

APPLE AND CINNAMON

Makes enough to fill twenty-five doughnuts

8 large Bramley apples, peeled, cored and cut into small pieces

200g soft light brown sugar

50ml water

1 cinnamon stick

juice and finely grated zest of 1 lemon

2 tsp ground cinnamon (optional)

Place the apples, sugar, water and cinnamon stick in a saucepan and set it over a low heat. Cook for 5 minutes, then add the lemon juice and zest. Cook for another 25 minutes, stirring occasionally, until the apples have collapsed into a purée.

If you are using the mixture to fill doughnuts, add the ground cinnamon to the sugar for dusting the doughnuts after frying them.

APPLE AND CINNAMON: ITS POSSIBILITIES

Pancakes
Ripple ice cream
Trifle
Tarts
Sponge cakes
Granola and yoghurt

LEMON CURD

Makes two jars

juice and finely grated zest of 6 lemons

200g unsalted butter, cut into small cubes

410g caster sugar

6 large eggs, lightly beaten

Place the lemon juice and zest in a large heatproof bowl with the butter and sugar. Set the bowl over a saucepan of simmering water, making sure the water doesn't touch the base of the bowl. Leave until the butter has melted, stirring occasionally, then whisk in the beaten eggs. Cook for about 10 minutes, whisking every 2–3 minutes, until the lemon curd has thickened. Watch the simmering water to make sure it doesn't boil rapidly or the eggs will curdle. Once the curd has thickened, strain it through a fine sieve, then pot in sterilised jars (see below) and seal. It will keep for up to 3 months in the fridge.

TO STERILISE JARS

Put some clamp-top preserving jars through a dishwasher cycle a couple of times. Place the lemon curd (or jam or mincemeat) in the jars and seal, then put the jars into a large, deep saucepan. Cover with water, bring to the boil and simmer for 15–20 minutes for a 450g jar, topping up the water if necessary.

LEMON CURD: ITS POSSIBILITIES

Pancakes
Ice cream
Lemon meringue pie
Sponge cakes
Tart
Profiteroles
Steamed puddings
Toast

RASPBERRY JAM

Makes two to three jars

900g jam sugar

1kg raspberries

juice of 2 lemons

Place the sugar in a roasting tin and warm gently in a low oven (about 140°C/Gas Mark 1) for 20 minutes. Meanwhile, place the raspberries and lemon juice in a large, heavy-based saucepan and bring to the boil over a low heat. Add the sugar and stir until dissolved. Simmer for 10–15 minutes or until setting point is reached. To test for setting point, place a plate in the fridge until cold, then place a small spoonful of jam on it. If you draw your finger through the jam, it should remain separated and not run back into the centre. As soon as the jam reaches setting point, spoon it into sterilised jars (see page 128) and seal.

RASPBERRY JAM: ITS POSSIBILITIES

Pancakes
Tarts
Toast
Sponge cakes
Queen of puddings
Ripple ice cream

PUDDINGS

STORE CUPBOARD

Prepare these at least two weeks before use; they will keep for ages.

A jar of Agen prunes covered in Earl Grey tea (just fill your jar with prunes, add a couple of Earl Grey teabags and a few strips of lemon zest, then cover with boiling water and seal the jar)

A jar of sultanas or raisins covered in Marc (fill a jar with sultanas or raisins, top up with Marc and seal)

HOT CHOCOLATE PUDDING

To serve eight

250g plain chocolate, with at least 70 per cent cocoa solids, cut into small chunks

250g unsalted butter, diced, plus extra for greasing

6 large eggs

5 large egg yolks

125g caster sugar, plus extra for dusting

75g plain flour

Here is a pudding that needs no introduction.

Grease 8 individual ramekins or dariole moulds (or one large ovenproof dish) with butter and dust with caster sugar.

Put the chocolate and butter in a heatproof bowl and place over a saucepan of simmering water, making sure the water doesn't touch the base of the bowl. Leave until melted. Meanwhile, using an electric mixer on full speed, whisk the eggs, yolks and sugar together for about 6 minutes, until they have at least tripled in volume.

Sift the flour into a bowl and slowly pour on the melted chocolate and butter mixture, whisking constantly until a thin paste has formed. Fold this into the whisked egg mixture very carefully but quickly, as the chocolate will start to set. Pour into the prepared dishes and bake in an oven preheated to 180°C/Gas Mark 4, until risen and firm on the outside but soft in the centre. The large one will take about 30 minutes to cook, the individual ones about 13 minutes. Serve with crème fraîche or ice cream and, if in season, some cherries.

CHOCOLATE BAKED ALASKA

To serve eight

a splash of good brandy

Chocolate Ice Cream
(see page 192)

GÉNOISE SPONGE

4 large eggs

125g caster sugar

125g plain flour,
sifted

50g unsalted
butter, melted

MERINGUE

3 large egg whites

240g caster sugar

With much research into chocolate ice cream, we had plenty of the stuff around, hence the Chocolate Baked Alaska. What could be finer than the white, fluffy exterior surrounding the dark middle?

First make the génoise sponge. Using an electric mixer, whisk the eggs and caster sugar on full speed for about 5 minutes, until tripled in volume. Fold the sifted flour though the mixture with a large metal spoon until completely incorporated, then fold in the melted butter. Pour into a parchment-lined 16 x 23cm baking tray, about 2.5cm deep, and place in an oven preheated to 160°C/Gas Mark 3. Bake for 25 minutes or until the sponge is firm to the touch and golden brown. Turn out on to a wire rack to cool.

Cut a circle out of the sponge about 20cm in diameter. Place it on a baking tray lined with baking parchment, then pour the brandy over it and leave for 1 hour.

Now make the meringue. Make sure your bowl and whisk are very clean before you start. Whisk the egg whites until they form stiff peaks, then gradually add the sugar, whisking until stiff and glossy.

Remove the chocolate ice cream from the freezer and pile it up on the sponge, leaving a 2.5cm border all round. Cover the whole Alaska with the meringue, starting from the rim of the sponge, then moving up over the ice cream. Place the Alaska in an oven preheated to 220°C/Gas Mark 7 for 8–10 minutes, until the meringue is golden brown. If you're worried the ice cream might be about to melt before the meringue is well coloured, insert a skewer and check that it comes out cold. Serve right away, with thick cream.

TREACLE TART

To serve twelve

1.1kg golden syrup
(and another 300g
up your sleeve)

juice and grated
zest of 2 lemons

2 tsp ground ginger

400g white breadcrumbs

PASTRY

315g soft unsalted butter

225g caster sugar

1 large egg

5 large egg yolks

560g strong white flour

Every cookbook, it would seem, has its Navaho Factor. To my shame, in book one it was the Treacle Tart. Fortunately I'm ready to meet the great chef in the sky, thanks to Justin remedying things in this new book.

First make the pastry. Cream the butter and sugar together until white and fluffy. Lightly beat together the egg and egg yolks, then add them to the mixture a little at a time in order to prevent curdling. Sift in the flour and mix until just incorporated. The pastry will be very soft, so wrap it in cling film and leave in the fridge overnight.

Take the pastry out of the fridge and let it soften at room temperature for 1–2 hours. Then cut it in half and roll out one piece on a lightly floured work surface to about 3mm thick (you won't need the other piece but it will keep well in the freezer). Use to line a 30cm loose-bottomed tart tin and chill for 1–2 hours. Then cover with cling film, fill with baking beans and bake in an oven preheated to 180°C/Gas Mark 4 for about 10 minutes, until golden brown around the edges. Remove the cling film and beans and return the pastry case to the oven until it is a good golden colour all over. Remove from the oven and leave to cool.

For the filling, put the golden syrup, lemon juice and zest and ground ginger in a pan and leave over a medium heat until hot. Stir in the breadcrumbs, remove from the heat and leave for about 10 minutes, until the golden syrup has been absorbed by the crumbs. Then add the extra golden syrup little by little until it starts to bleed out of the breadcrumbs; you might not need to add all the syrup. Pour the filling into the tart case and bake at 180°C/Gas Mark 4 for 30–45 minutes, until golden brown. Serve with extra-thick Jersey cream.

QUEEN OF PUDDINGS

To serve four to six

60g *white breadcrumbs*

60g *sponge cake crumbs*

grated zest of 1 lemon

a pinch of freshly grated nutmeg

190g *caster sugar*

1 *vanilla pod*

700ml *full-fat milk*

30g *unsalted butter*

4 *large eggs, separated*

a good dollop of Raspberry Jam (see page 130)

May I say, this is a very lovely pudding indeed. The way they pipe the meringue on at St. John has the effect of a sea of white bosoms with little brown nipples. This may be to do with my foetid imagination, and not to do with the effect the pastry section is after.

Put the breadcrumbs in a large bowl with the sponge crumbs, lemon zest, nutmeg and 30g of the sugar.

Slit the vanilla pod open lengthways and scrape out the seeds. Place the pod and seeds in a pan with the milk and butter and heat until warm. Pour the milk over the breadcrumb mixture and leave to stand for 15 minutes, then stir in the egg yolks. Pour the mixture into a large ovenproof serving dish and place in a roasting tin half-filled with hot water. Bake in an oven preheated to 160°C/Gas Mark 3 for 25–30 minutes, until firm to the touch. Remove from the oven and leave to cool for about 10 minutes.

Meanwhile, whisk the egg whites until they form stiff peaks, then gradually whisk in the remaining sugar.

Spread a very large dollop of raspberry jam over the baked mixture, being careful not to break the surface. You can either pipe the meringue on or just spoon it on top. Bake at 200°C/Gas Mark 6 for 8–10 minutes, until golden brown. Serve piping hot, with pouring cream.

BITTER CHOCOLATE CREAM

To serve six

250g plain chocolate, with at least 70 per cent cocoa solids (we use an El Rey Venezuelan chocolate called Apamate, at 73.5 per cent)

1 gelatine leaf

375ml double cream

125ml full-fat milk

100g caster sugar

Cor blimey!

Cut the chocolate into small chunks, put it in a large bowl and set aside. Put the gelatine leaf in a separate bowl and cover with cold water.

Pour the cream and milk into a saucepan, add the caster sugar and bring slowly to the boil, whisking occasionally. Now go back to your gelatine and squeeze out the water. Once the cream is boiling, take it off the heat, add the squeezed-out gelatine leaf and whisk until dissolved. Then strain the hot cream mixture over the chocolate and whisk until the chocolate has dissolved. You will have a beautiful, glossy chocolate cream.

Pour the mixture into 6 individual moulds or one large serving dish and leave in the fridge for 4–6 hours, until set. Serve with Hazelnut Biscuits (see page 119) and tea-soaked prunes (see page 134), or with cherries when in season.

DAMSON JELLY

To serve four

500g damsons

100ml water

125g caster sugar

leaf gelatine

Jelly doesn't fail to please. No one can resist that wobble.

Place the damsons in a heavy-based saucepan, add the water and sugar and bring to the boil, stirring to dissolve the sugar. Simmer gently until the damsons are soft. (You can also do this in the oven in a deep roasting tin but bring the water and sugar to the boil first and pour them over the damsons. Cover with foil and bake at 160°C/Gas Mark 3.)

Let the damsons cool and then leave in the fridge for 2 days; this seems a long time but it produces a really well-flavoured juice.

After 2 days, strain the juice from the damsons, set the damsons aside and measure the juice; you should have about 600ml, for which you will need 3 gelatine leaves. Soak the gelatine leaves in cold water for about 8 minutes. Meanwhile, heat 300ml of the damson juice until hot. Squeeze the water out of the gelatine leaves, add them to the hot damson juice and whisk until dissolved. Then whisk into the rest of the juice and pour through a fine sieve into a jelly mould. Leave in the fridge overnight to set.

Serve with some of the poached damsons, plus whipped cream and Madeleines (see page 116).

POACHED DAMSONS: THEIR POSSIBILITIES

Hot with vanilla ice cream
Crumbles
Tarts
Yoghurt and granola
Fool
Ripple ice cream

APPLE AND CALVADOS TRIFLE

To serve six to eight

3 large Bramley apples,
peeled, cored and
roughly chopped

3 Cox apples,
peeled, cored and
roughly chopped

2 tbsp soft light
brown sugar

½ tsp ground cinnamon

at least 6 tbsp Calvados

SPONGE

4 large eggs

125g caster sugar

125g plain flour, sifted

CUSTARD

450ml double cream

1 tsp vanilla extract

2 large eggs

2 large egg yolks

85g caster sugar

Gone are the hundreds and thousands, the boring jelly, the tinned fruit. Trifle has found its perch again.

First prepare the sponge. Whisk the eggs and sugar on high speed with an electric mixer for 3–4 minutes, until tripled in volume. Slowly fold in the sifted flour, then pour into a Swiss roll tin lined with baking parchment. Place in an oven preheated to 160°C/Gas Mark 3 and bake for about 25 minutes, until golden brown and firm to the touch. Turn out on to a wire rack to cool.

Place the Bramleys and Cox apples in a saucepan with the sugar and cinnamon. Cook over a medium heat until the apples are tender, then set aside to cool.

To make the custard, pour the double cream and vanilla extract into a saucepan and bring to the boil. Meanwhile, mix the eggs, egg yolks and sugar together in a large bowl. Once the cream reaches boiling point, pour it over the egg mixture, whisking constantly to prevent the eggs scrambling. Strain though a fine sieve into a large heatproof bowl, then place the bowl over a pan of simmering water. Whisk occasionally until the custard has thickened. Pour through a fine sieve into a plastic container, leave to cool, then chill.

ALMONDS

100g flaked almonds

30g icing sugar

1 tbsp Calvados

CREAM

300ml double cream

30g icing sugar

1 tsp vanilla extract

Mix the almonds, icing sugar and Calvados together in a bowl, then spread them out on a baking tray. Toast in an oven preheated to 180°C/ Gas Mark 4 for 6–8 minutes, until golden brown.

For the cream, whisk the double cream, icing sugar and vanilla extract together until soft peaks are formed, then place in the fridge.

To assemble the trifle, you will need a large glass bowl. Cut the sponge into slices 2cm thick (nothing worse than not enough booze-soaked sponge) and place in the bottom of your bowl. Then pour on at least 6 tablespoons of Calvados and leave for 30 minutes to soak in. Cover with the apple mixture, then the thick custard, then the cream. Each layer should be roughly the same thickness. Top with the sugared roasted almonds.

SUMMER PUDDING

To serve six to eight

250g caster sugar

1 litre water

250g strawberries

250g raspberries

250g redcurrants

*1 Sandwich Loaf
(see page 102)*

I am not a fan of individual summer puddings, as there is always too much bread and not enough fruit. That's why we make our summer puddings to serve at least two.

Put the sugar and water in a large saucepan and bring to the boil, stirring to dissolve the sugar. Simmer for 5 minutes. Add the strawberries, bring back to a simmer, then take off the heat and add the raspberries and redcurrants. Pour the mixture into a plastic container and leave to cool, then place in the fridge overnight (leaving it this long means that plenty of juices will leach out of the fruit).

Line a 2.3 litre pudding basin with cling film, leaving plenty overhanging. Cut the crusts off the bread and slice it about 8mm thick. Use the bread to line the sides of the basin, squeezing the slices in so there are no gaps. Then cut a disc to cover the bottom of the basin and a larger disc that will fit the top. Place the small disc in the basin and pour the fruit into it, filling it right to the top and including as much juice as possible. Place the larger disc of bread on top, pull up the excess cling film to seal all the juices in and tie the ends in a knot. Return any leftover fruit or juice to the fridge.

Put the basin in a deep plastic tray and weight the pudding down by placing a flat tray on it and then putting something heavy on top of that – tins of food will do nicely. Then leave overnight in the fridge.

To serve, turn the pudding out on to a large serving dish and pour some of the remaining juice over it. Accompany with a bowl of extra-thick Jersey cream.

YOU CAN SERVE ANY LEFTOVER FRUIT WITH:

Meringues and cream
Yoghurt and granola
Custard

Or turn it into a fool

YOU CAN TURN ANY LEFTOVER JUICE INTO:

Jellies
Ices

Or add a few drops to a glass of Champagne

BLACK HAT

To serve six to eight

The black hat is basically an autumnal summer pudding, so the rules about size still apply.

Make as for Summer Pudding (see page 150) but increase the amount of sugar to 320g, replace the strawberries with 250g plums (stoned), and the other fruit with 250g blackberries, 250g blackcurrants and 100g elderberries.

QUINCE AND PRUNES

To serve four

2 litres water

500g caster sugar

6 large quinces

12 prunes
(Agen, if possible)

I think it is vital to get prunes with their stones in, which gives them structure to swell with joy but maintain their prune dignity.

Place the water and sugar in a saucepan and bring to the boil, stirring occasionally to help the sugar to dissolve.

Meanwhile, peel the quinces but keep the skin and put to one side. Cut the quinces into quarters, remove the cores and keep these also. Lay the peel and cores in a large, deep roasting dish (their pigment turns the quinces that lovely ruby colour), cover with a sheet of baking parchment, then put the quinces on top.

When the water and sugar mixture comes to the boil, pour it over the quinces and cover with baking parchment. Weight down with a couple of heavy plates, then cover with foil. Place in an oven preheated to 140°C/Gas Mark 1 and bake for 4–5 hours, until the quinces are soft. Remove the foil, plates and parchment, add the prunes, then cover with foil again and leave to cool.

Serve hot, with either pouring cream or Vanilla Ice Cream (see page 190). They're also great just on their own.

QUINCE AND PRUNES: THEIR POSSIBILITIES

Jellies, with all that lovely juice
(remember, 3 leaves of gelatine per 600ml)
Crumbles
Tarts
Strudel (cheers, Lee)
Pies

YOU FOOL

To serve two

200g blackberries, or
any fruit you desire

50g caster sugar

400ml double cream

Who are you calling a fool?

Put the fruit in a pan with half the sugar and cook very gently for a few minutes (if you use tart fruit such as rhubarb, you will need more sugar). All you are looking to do with the fruit is soften it until the juices start to run. If the fruit is really ripe you won't even need to cook it – just mix it with the sugar and crush lightly with a fork.

Leave the fruit to cool. Whip the cream with the rest of the sugar until it forms soft peaks, then fold in the fruit. Serve with Shortbread (see page 117).

RHUBARB CRUMBLE CAKE

To serve six to eight

3 large sticks of rhubarb

50g caster sugar

50g Demerara sugar

grated zest of 1 orange

CAKE MIX

125g soft unsalted butter

125g caster sugar

3 large eggs,
lightly beaten

160g self-raising
flour, sifted

50ml full-fat milk

CRUMBLE MIX

125g plain flour

95g unsalted butter,
cut into small cubes

60g Demerara sugar

30g ground almonds

30g flaked almonds

a pinch of salt

This is having your cake and eating it.

First top and tail the rhubarb, give it a good wash and cut it into slices about 2cm thick. Mix it with the sugars and the orange zest and set aside for 30 minutes.

For the cake mix, cream the butter and sugar together until light and fluffy. Gradually add the beaten eggs, bit by bit to prevent curdling. Then fold in the sifted flour and last of all mix in the milk. Put to one side.

For the crumble mix, sift the flour into a bowl, add the butter and rub them together with your fingertips until they look like large breadcrumbs. Stir in the Demerara sugar, ground almonds, flaked almonds and salt.

Butter a deep 20cm springform cake tin and line the base and sides with baking parchment. Spread the cake mix evenly over the base of the tin, then place the rhubarb on top. Sprinkle the crumble mix over the rhubarb. Place in an oven pre-heated to 180°C/Gas Mark 4 and bake for about 1½ hours, covering the top loosely with foil if it gets too dark. The cake is ready when a skewer inserted in the centre comes out clean. Serve warm, with custard or extra-thick Jersey cream.

YOU DO NOT HAVE TO USE RHUBARB,
YOU COULD USE:

Apples
Apricots
Quinces (you will need to cook them first)
Nectarines
Gooseberries
Pears and ginger
Plums
Damsons

PROFITEROLES STUFFED WITH VANILLA ICE CREAM

To serve eight

250ml water

100g unsalted butter, diced

140g strong white flour

a pinch of salt

2 tsp caster sugar

5 large eggs, lightly beaten

Vanilla Ice Cream (see page 190)

HOT CHOCOLATE SAUCE

500g plain chocolate, with at least 70 per cent cocoa solids, broken into chunks

700ml water

120g caster sugar

Vanilla ice cream and chocolate sauce are a match made in heaven, but then add the rigour of the pastry ...

Place the water and butter in a deep, heavy-based saucepan and bring to the boil – do this slowly, so the butter will just have melted by the time the water is boiling. Remove from the heat and immediately stir in the flour, salt and sugar. Return the pan to a medium heat and beat with a wooden spoon until the mixture becomes smooth and no longer sticks to the sides of the pan. Leave to cool for 3–4 minutes, then gradually beat in the eggs one at a time, until the mixture is shiny and thick enough to drop reluctantly from the spoon. Cover with cling film and leave to cool.

Line a baking sheet with baking parchment. Fill a piping bag with the mixture and pipe it on to the baking tray in balls 1.5cm in diameter. The profiteroles will spread, so be sure to allow a little room between each one.

Bake in an oven preheated to 220°C/Gas Mark 7 for 20–25 minutes, until crisp and golden brown. Remove from the oven and leave to cool on a wire rack.

For the hot chocolate sauce, place all the ingredients in a heavy-based saucepan and bring slowly to the boil. Pass through a fine sieve.

To serve, slice the profiteroles widthways through the middle and fill with vanilla ice cream. Serve with a jug of piping-hot chocolate sauce.

RICE PUDDING WITH MARC
AND RAISIN CUSTARD

To serve six

125g unsalted butter

150g caster sugar

200g pudding rice

1.5 litres full-fat milk

300ml double cream

1 vanilla pod

a pinch of salt

MARC AND
RAISIN CUSTARD

150ml full-fat milk

300ml double cream

1 vanilla pod

3 large egg yolks

60g caster sugar

60g raisins soaked in
Marc (see page 134)

Rice pudding, custard and Marc. Where can we go wrong?

Place the butter and sugar in a large, heavy-based casserole and melt over a medium heat, stirring occasionally. Bring to the boil and let it bubble, without stirring, until it turns into a golden brown caramel. Add the rice and stir to combine it with the caramel, then add the milk and cream. Once the liquid hits the caramel, the caramel will become hard and stringy. Don't worry; as the liquid heats up, the caramel will melt into it and become smooth again. Slit the vanilla pod open lengthways, scrape out the seeds and add the seeds and pod to the rice, together with the pinch of salt. Bring to the boil and place in an oven preheated to 160°C/Gas Mark 3. Bake for 1½–2 hours, until golden brown on top and thick and creamy.

To make the custard, pour the milk and cream into a saucepan. Slit the vanilla pod open lengthways, scrape out the seeds and add the pod and seeds to the pan. Bring to the boil.

Whisk the egg yolks and sugar together in a bowl.

Pour the boiling milk over the egg yolk mixture, whisking constantly to prevent curdling. Then pour it back into the saucepan and cook over a low heat, stirring constantly with a wooden spoon, until it has thickened enough to coat the back of the spoon. Strain through a fine sieve into a bowl and add the soaked raisins.

To serve, spoon the hot rice pudding into deep bowls and pour the custard on top, making sure everyone gets a fair amount of Marc-soaked raisins (which are like little pockets of joy).

BURNT SHEEP'S MILK YOGHURT

To serve six

10 large egg yolks

100g caster sugar, plus extra for sprinkling

150ml full-fat milk

500ml sheep's milk yoghurt

A little musk of farmyard in your pudding.

Place the egg yolks and sugar in a bowl and whisk for about a minute, until well combined. Pour the milk into a saucepan and bring to the boil. Pour the boiling milk over the egg yolk mixture, whisking constantly to prevent curdling. Then add the sheep's milk yoghurt and whisk well.

Pass the mixture through a fine sieve and pour into 6 ramekins or china moulds. Place them in a roasting tin and pour in enough boiling water to come half way up the sides of the dishes. Place the tray in an oven preheated to 160°C/Gas Mark 3 and bake for 30–45 minutes, until the custards are set around the sides and still wobble a little in the middle. You must take them out of the oven with the wobble, as the residual heat will finish the cooking. Take the ramekins out of the roasting tin and let them cool for 1 hour, then place in the fridge for 2 hours.

Just before serving, sprinkle caster sugar over the top of the custards – just enough to cover the surface – then caramelise the sugar with a blowtorch or under a grill (a blowtorch gives a better result). Serve on their own or with Shortbread (see page 117).

BAKED GOAT'S CURD CHEESECAKE

To serve ten to twelve

1kg goat's curd

juice and grated zest of 2 lemons

7 large eggs

250g caster sugar

1 bottle of Marc de Gewurztraminer d'Alsace

I like the way the recipe says one bottle of Marc, taking into account the chef's needs. Cheesecake may have left you uninspired before ... Ah! Cheesecakes, they are a-changing.

You can find goat's curd at good cheese shops, such as Neal's Yard Dairy.

Place the goat's curd in a large mixing bowl, add the lemon juice and zest and whisk together with a balloon whisk until light and fluffy. The goat's curd has a tendency to get stuck in the whisk but don't be tempted to use an electric mixer as it will overwork the curd.

Whisk together the eggs and sugar just for a minute, then add them little by little to the goat's curd mixture, whisking constantly. Pour the mixture into a 25cm springform cake tin lined with baking parchment and put it on a baking tray. Place in an oven preheated to 180°C/Gas Mark 4 and bake for about 1 hour, until golden brown. It will still have a good wobble when it comes out of the oven but don't worry, it will set as it cools down.

To serve, cut the cheesecake into slices and pour 1–2 tablespoons of Marc over each one.

STEADYING PUDDINGS

BLACK CAP

To serve six

1 quantity of
Rice Pudding
(see page 164 – omit
the custard)

150g tea-soaked prunes
(see page 134)

2 tbsp Armagnac

At the risk of repeating myself, come on, rice pudding and prunes. I don't need to spell it out.

Make the rice pudding as described on page 164, then leave to go cold.

Line a 2.3 litre pudding basin with cling film, letting the ends hang over the sides. Drain any excess liquid from the prunes, then place them in the basin and pour the Armagnac over them. Spoon in the cold rice pudding, filling the bowl right to the top, and cover with the overhanging ends of the cling film. Chill for 3–4 hours.

To serve, turn out the Black Cap on to a plate and accompany with custard or pouring cream.

APPLE AND BLACKBERRY COBBLER

To serve six

6 Bramley apples, peeled, cored and finely chopped

50g unsalted butter

75g soft light brown sugar

juice and grated zest of 1 lemon

250g blackberries

1 egg, beaten, to glaze

Demerara sugar, for sprinkling

DOUGH

225g self-raising flour

100g unsalted butter, diced

50g caster sugar

juice and grated zest of ½ lemon

1 large egg, lightly beaten

about 50ml full-fat milk

My Mum still remembers lying in bed and hearing the sound of the mill workers' clogs on the cobbled streets of Bolton. Excuse me, I digress.

To make the dough, sift the flour into a bowl and rub in the butter with your fingertips until the mixture resembles breadcrumbs. Stir in the sugar, lemon juice and zest, then mix in the beaten egg. Add enough milk to make a soft, pliable dough. Wrap in cling film and leave to rest in the fridge for 3–4 hours.

While the dough rests, make the filling. Put the apples in a saucepan with the butter, sugar, lemon juice and zest and cook over a gentle heat until tender. Remove from the heat and stir in the blackberries. Pour the mixture into a baking dish about 25cm square.

Roll out the dough to 1cm thick and use a pastry cutter to cut out rounds 2cm in diameter. Place them on top of the fruit – they should cover it completely. Brush the top of the cobbler with the beaten egg and sprinkle with Demerara sugar. Place in an oven preheated to 180°C/Gas Mark 4 and bake for about 30 minutes, until the topping is golden brown. Serve hot, with custard or extra-thick Jersey cream.

INSTEAD OF BLACKBERRY AND APPLE
YOU COULD USE:

Rhubarb
Pear
Quince
Damson
Gooseberry

BREAD PUDDING

To serve eight

250g stale white bread
(e.g. the Sandwich
Loaf on page 102)

65g fresh minced
beef suet

130g soft dark
brown sugar

20g finely chopped
mixed candied peel

55g raisins

30g currants

25g sultanas

25g Bramley apples,
peeled, cored and diced

1 large egg

1½ tsp ground mixed
spice

½ tsp ground allspice

2 tbsp dark rum

15g unsalted butter, cut
into small dice

Demerara sugar, for
sprinkling

Never waste yesterday's bread.

Cut the crusts off the bread, then rip it into small pieces and place in a bowl. Cover with water and leave to soak for 25 minutes.

Put all the remaining ingredients except the butter and Demerara sugar in a large bowl and mix with a wooden spoon for 3–4 minutes, until thoroughly combined. Squeeze all the excess water out of the soaked bread – come on, a really big squeeze – then add the bread to the rest of the ingredients. Mix well for another 3–4 minutes. The mixture will be very wet. Transfer to an ovenproof serving dish, cover with the pieces of butter and sprinkle Demerara sugar on top. Place in an oven preheated to 180°C/Gas Mark 4 and bake for 1½ hours, until golden brown.

BUTTERSCOTCH SAUCE

250g caster sugar

600ml double cream

125g unsalted butter, cut into small dice

Meanwhile, make the butterscotch sauce. Put the sugar into a heavy-based saucepan with 2 tablespoons of water and melt over a low heat, tilting the pan occasionally so the sugar melts evenly. Then raise the heat and cook, without stirring, until it turns into a golden-brown caramel. Slowly pour in the cream, being careful as the hot caramel will spit. Turn the heat down low and let the caramel dissolve slowly into the cream. Remove from the heat and whisk in the butter, a few pieces at a time. Strain through a fine sieve into a bowl.

Serve the Bread Pudding hot, accompanied by Vanilla Ice Cream (see page 190) and the Butterscotch sauce.

STICKY DATE PUDDING

To serve eight

220g stoned dates

1 single espresso

375ml water

1 tsp bicarbonate of soda

65g soft unsalted butter

225g soft dark
brown sugar

3 large eggs,
lightly beaten

225g plain flour, sifted

Butterscotch Sauce
(see page 177)

Uh huh!

Put the dates, coffee and water in a large saucepan and bring to the boil. Remove from the heat and add the bicarbonate of soda. It will fizz and fizz, but wait until it stops fizzing and then stir everything together. Leave for a couple of hours, or ideally overnight in the fridge so the dates can absorb most of the liquid.

Using an electric mixer, cream the butter and sugar together for about 5 minutes, until light and fluffy. Gradually mix in the beaten eggs, then the sifted flour. Add the date mixture. The mix will now be very runny but don't worry, it will set during baking, and produce a very moist sponge.

Pour the sponge mix into a greased 1.7 litre pudding basin; it should be about three-quarters full. Cover the mixture with a circle of baking parchment, then place a piece of foil (with a generous pleat in the middle) over the basin and secure with string. Put the basin in a deep roasting tin and pour enough hot water into the tin to come half way up the sides of the basin. Steam in an oven preheated to 160°C/Gas Mark 3 for about 1½ hours, until the pudding is well risen and firm to the touch (remember to keep the water topped up).

Turn out into a large serving bowl and pour hot Butter-scotch Sauce over the top. Serve with a generous helping of chilled double cream or Vanilla Ice Cream (see page 190).

GINGERBREAD PUDDING

To serve eight

90g stale white bread

175g plain flour

90g ground almonds

175g fresh minced beef suet

25g baking powder

a pinch of salt

1½ tsp ground ginger

1 tsp ground mixed spice

2 large eggs

175g stem ginger in syrup

2 tbsp grated fresh root ginger

3 tbsp grated apple

180g golden syrup

180g black treacle

150ml full-fat milk

Butterscotch Sauce, to serve (see page 177)

Remember gingerbread when you were young? Well forget it, you've just grown up.

Cut the crusts off the bread, then rip it into 2cm pieces and place in a large mixing bowl. Sift the flour over the bread, then add all the rest of the ingredients. Stir together for about 4 minutes until thoroughly combined.

Butter and flour a 2.3 litre pudding basin and spoon in the mixture; the basin should be about three-quarters full. Cover the mixture with a circle of baking parchment, then place a piece of foil (with a generous pleat in the middle) over the basin and secure with string. Put the basin in a deep roasting tin and pour enough hot water into the tin to come half way up the sides of the basin. Steam in an oven preheated to 160°C/Gas Mark 3 for 1½ hours (remember to keep the water topped up). Turn out on to a serving dish and cover with hot Butterscotch Sauce. Serve some Vanilla Ice Cream (see page 190) on the side.

VICTORIA PUDDING

To serve six

160g unsalted butter

120g caster sugar

40g soft light
brown sugar

grated zest of 1 lemon

3 eggs, lightly beaten

240g plain flour

a pinch of salt

10g baking powder

about 100ml
full-fat milk

Demerara sugar, for
sprinkling

FILLING

12 Victoria plums
(nice and ripe),
halved and stoned

60g caster sugar

2 tbsp quetsch
(plum brandy)

Gastronomically as exciting as a Prince Albert.

For the filling, place the plums and sugar in a saucepan and heat very slowly, just to dissolve the sugar. Remove from the heat, add the quetsch and set aside.

Cream the butter, sugars and lemon zest together until pale and fluffy, then beat in the eggs, adding them little by little to prevent curdling. Sift in the flour, salt and baking powder and fold in thoroughly. Add enough milk to give a mixture that drops reluctantly from the spoon.

Arrange the plums over the base of an ovenproof serving dish about 25cm square. Cover with the sponge mix, then sprinkle Demerara sugar on top. Place in an oven preheated to 180°C/Gas Mark 4 and bake for about 30 minutes, until the pudding is golden brown and a skewer inserted in the centre comes out clean. It will rise quite a lot, so make sure it's not too near the top of the oven. Serve hot, with double cream or custard.

BRIGADE PUDDING

To serve eight

MINCEMEAT

*3 large quinces, cooked
as for Quince and
Prunes (see page 153)*

*2 Cox apples, peeled,
cored and diced*

*4 Bramley apples,
peeled, cored and diced*

*250g fresh minced
beef suet*

440g raisins

440g currants

440g sultanas

*135g chopped candied
mixed peel*

*440g soft dark
brown sugar*

*juice and grated
zest of 3 oranges*

*juice and grated
zest of 3 lemons*

*5 tsp ground
mixed spice*

When I stayed the weekend with Tanya and Piers Thompson, she produced this delicious pudding, somewhat reminiscent of a bee's bottom with stripes of suet pastry and mincemeat. As well as being a dab hand at pastry, Tanya is a joy to dance with.

To make the mincemeat, mix together all the ingredients except the Armagnac and place on a large plastic tray. Cover and leave in a cool, dark place (not the fridge) for 2 days, mixing two or three times a day.

Transfer the mixture to a large roasting tray, cover with foil and bake in an oven preheated to 140°C/Gas Mark 1 for around 4–5 hours, until the suet has melted and is bubbling and the mixture has darkened. Remove from the oven and leave to cool, stirring every 10 minutes to make sure the fruit is covered by the fat. This helps to preserve the mincemeat. Finally, when cool, add a very generous slosh of Armagnac (about 300ml). Pot in sterilised jars (see page 128) and seal. It will make about 2kg, so there will be plenty of mincemeat left for making mince pies at Christmas.

2 tsp ground allspice

1 tsp ground mace

2 tsp ground cinnamon

100g slivered almonds

*and a nice bottle
of Armagnac
up your sleeve*

SUET PASTRY

500g self-raising flour

a pinch of salt

250g fresh minced
beef suet

250–300ml
full-fat milk, warmed

For the pastry, sift the flour and salt into a bowl and rub in the minced suet. Pour in 250ml of the milk and mix until a soft dough is formed, adding a little more milk if necessary. Wrap in cling film and leave to rest in the fridge for 1 hour.

Roll out the suet pastry to 1cm thick, then cut it into 5 discs as follows: 7cm diameter, 9cm diameter, 11cm diameter, 13cm diameter and 15cm diameter. Butter and flour a 2 litre pudding basin, then start to assemble the pudding. First, place the smallest disc of suet pastry at the bottom of the basin. Follow that with a layer of mincemeat 1cm thick, then with the next round of suet pastry and another 1cm-thick layer of mincemeat. Carry on until you reach the top of the basin, finishing with suet pastry. Put a circle of baking parchment on top, then cover the basin with a piece of foil (with a generous pleat in the middle) and secure with string. Put it in a deep roasting tin and pour enough hot water into the tin to come half way up the sides of the basin.

Steam in an oven preheated to 160°C/Gas Mark 3 for about 2½ hours, until golden brown and bubbling hot (remember to keep the water topped up). Turn out and serve hot, with custard or extra-thick Jersey cream.

PRUNE AND SUET PUDDING

To serve six

450g Agen prunes
(with the stones in)

50g unsalted butter

150ml Vieille Prune
*(plus some more
up your sleeve)*

grated zest of 1 lemon

SUET PASTRY

250g self-raising flour

a pinch of salt

125g fresh minced
beef suet

125–150ml
full-fat milk, warmed

1 egg, lightly beaten

A match made in heaven.

Mix all the ingredients for the filling together and leave overnight.

To make the suet pastry, sift the flour and salt into a bowl, then rub in the suet. Pour in 125ml of the milk and mix until a soft dough is formed, adding a little more milk if necessary. Wrap in cling film and leave to rest in the fridge for 1 hour.

Butter and flour a 1.2 litre pudding basin. Roll out two-thirds of the suet pastry to 1cm thick and use to line the pudding basin, leaving plenty overhanging the edge. Fill the basin with the prune mixture and add an extra splash of Vieille Prune for good measure. Roll out the remaining pastry and cut a round that will fit the top of the basin. Use it to cover the filling and brush the edges with beaten egg to seal. Trim off the surplus pastry so there is only 1cm left overhanging. Seal the overhanging pastry and lid together.

Place a round of baking parchment on top of the pastry and then cover the basin with a piece of foil (with a generous pleat in the middle) and secure with a piece of string.

Put the basin in a deep roasting tin and pour enough hot water into the tin to come half way up the sides of the basin. Steam in an oven preheated to 160°C/Gas Mark 3 for about 2½ hours, until golden brown on top and piping hot in the middle (remember to keep the water topped up). Turn out and serve with a generous helping of chilled double cream.

STEAMED LEMON AND VANILLA SYRUP SPONGE

To serve four to six

1 vanilla pod

1 lemon

140g unsalted butter

125g caster sugar

3 eggs, lightly beaten

200g plain flour

1½ tsp baking powder

100–150ml full-fat milk

SYRUP

juice and grated zest
of 2 lemons

200g caster sugar

150ml water

Keep the scurvy at bay.

Slit the vanilla pod open lengthways and scrape out the seeds, reserving the pod. Zest the lemon. Cream together the butter, sugar, lemon zest and vanilla seeds until light and fluffy, then gradually add the beaten eggs. Sift in the flour and baking powder and fold in thoroughly. Add enough milk to give a soft dropping consistency, then set aside.

To make the syrup, put the lemon juice and zest in a small saucepan with the sugar, water and the reserved vanilla pod. Heat gently, stirring until the sugar has dissolved, then bring to the boil and simmer until the mixture has a syrupy consistency.

Cut the zested lemon in half widthways and trim off the bottom and top. Place the widest end of one of the lemon halves in a buttered and floured 1.2 litre pudding basin and cover with the syrup, reserving a little for later. Spoon in the sponge mix. Place a round of baking parchment on top, cover the basin with a piece of foil (with a generous pleat in the middle) and secure with string. Put the basin in a deep roasting tin and pour enough hot water into the tin to come half way up the sides of the basin. Steam in an oven preheated to 160°C/Gas Mark 3 for about 2 hours, until well risen and firm to the touch (remember to keep the water topped up). Turn out into a large serving bowl and pour the last of the syrup over the top. Serve with double cream.

ICE CREAM

VANILLA ICE CREAM

Makes 1 litre

2 vanilla pods

375ml full-fat milk

450ml double cream

5 large egg yolks

150g caster sugar

Where would we be without it?

Slit the vanilla pods open lengthways and scrape out the seeds. Put the seeds and pods in a heavy-based saucepan with the milk and cream and bring slowly to the boil to infuse the vanilla. Meanwhile, place the egg yolks and sugar in a large bowl and whisk together for a couple of minutes.

Pour the boiling milk over the egg yolk mixture, whisking constantly to prevent curdling, then return the mixture to the saucepan. Cook over a low heat, stirring constantly with a wooden spoon, until it thickens enough to coat the back of the spoon. Pour through a fine sieve into a plastic container and cool down quickly in an ice bath (a large bowl filled with ice cubes is fine). Leave in the fridge overnight, then churn in an ice-cream machine.

TREACLE TOFFEE ICE CREAM

Makes 1 litre

375ml full-fat milk

450ml double cream

5 large egg yolks

125g caster sugar

TREACLE TOFFEE

250g black treacle

250g Demerara sugar

60g unsalted butter

Aah baby, let's slip into something a bit colder.

To make the treacle toffee, place all the ingredients in a deep, heavy-based saucepan and bring slowly to the boil, stirring to dissolve the sugar. Simmer for about an hour, until thick and glossy, stirring frequently. Pour the mixture on to an oiled metal tray and leave to cool. Break into small chunks and place them in an airtight container (you'll only need half the toffee for this recipe but the rest will keep well).

Pour the milk and cream into a heavy-based saucepan and bring slowly to the boil. Meanwhile, place the egg yolks and sugar in a large bowl and whisk together for a couple of minutes. Pour in the boiling milk, whisking constantly to prevent curdling, then return the mixture to the saucepan. Cook over a low heat, stirring constantly with a wooden spoon, until the mixture has thickened enough to coat the back of the spoon. Pour through a fine sieve into a plastic container and whisk in half the treacle toffee until dissolved. Cool down quickly in an ice bath (a large bowl filled with ice cubes is fine), then leave in the fridge overnight. Churn in an ice-cream machine.

CHOCOLATE ICE CREAM

Makes 1 litre

200g plain chocolate,
with at least 70 per cent
cocoa solids (we use an
El Rey Venezuelan
chocolate called
Apamate, at
73.5 per cent)

6 large egg yolks

115g caster sugar

500ml full-fat milk

50ml double cream

40g good-quality
cocoa powder

CARAMEL

70g caster sugar

75ml water

We finally did it, battling with the schizophrenic nature of chocolate – the sweetness going in one direction, the chocolate taste in another, plus the chalkiness of bitter chocolate. The battle was worthwhile and we now have the perfect chocolate ice cream. I hope you'll agree.

Chop the chocolate into small pieces and place in a bowl set over a pan of simmering water, making sure the water doesn't touch the base of the bowl. Leave to melt.

Put the egg yolks and caster sugar in a separate bowl and whisk with an electric beater for about 5 minutes, until the mixture is thick enough to leave a trail on the surface when the whisk is lifted.

Place the milk, cream and cocoa powder in a heavy-based saucepan and bring slowly to the boil, whisking occasionally to prevent the cocoa powder sticking to the bottom of the saucepan. Pour it over the egg yolk mixture, whisking constantly to prevent curdling. Then return the mixture to the saucepan and add the melted chocolate. Cook over a low heat for around 8 minutes, stirring constantly. Remove from the heat and set aside.

To make the caramel, place the sugar and water in a small, deep, heavy-based saucepan and bring slowly to the boil, stirring to dissolve the sugar. Raise the heat and simmer, without stirring, until a very dark caramel is achieved. Remove from the heat and whisk the hot caramel into the ice cream base a little at a time.

Pour through a fine sieve into a plastic container, then cool down quickly in an ice bath (a large bowl filled with ice cubes is fine). Leave in the fridge for 2 days before churning in an ice-cream machine. Once churned, leave for 3–4 days before eating. I know this might prove difficult but it does improve in flavour.

RIPPLE ICE CREAM

Makes 1 litre

1 vanilla pod

375ml full-fat milk

450ml double cream

5 large egg yolks

155g caster sugar

about 500g fruit purée, jam or sauce – Raspberry Jam (see page 130) or Butterscotch Sauce (see page 177) work well

Who can resist a ripple?

Slit the vanilla pod open lengthways and scrape out the seeds. Put the seeds and pod in a heavy-based saucepan with the milk and cream and bring slowly to the boil to infuse the vanilla. Meanwhile, place the egg yolks and sugar in a large bowl and whisk together for a couple of minutes.

Pour the boiling milk over the egg yolk mixture, whisking constantly to prevent curdling, then return the mixture to the saucepan. Cook over a low heat, stirring constantly with a wooden spoon, until it thickens enough to coat the back of the spoon.

Pour through a fine sieve into a plastic container and cool down quickly in an ice bath (a large bowl filled with ice cubes is fine). Leave in the fridge overnight, then churn in an ice-cream machine. When it's almost frozen, ripple your chosen flavour though the ice cream.

SULTANA AND MARC
ICE CREAM

Makes 1 litre

375ml full-fat milk

450ml double cream

5 large egg yolks

130g caster sugar

100g sultanas soaked in Marc (see page 134)

Ice cream ... Way hay!

Pour the milk and cream into a heavy-based saucepan and bring slowly to the boil. Meanwhile, put the egg yolks and sugar into a large bowl and whisk together for a couple of minutes. Pour in the boiling milk, whisking constantly to prevent curdling. Then pour the mixture back into the saucepan and return to a low heat. Cook, stirring constantly with a wooden spoon, until the custard thickens enough to coat the back of the spoon; don't let it boil or it will curdle.

Pour through a fine sieve into a plastic container and stir in the sultanas and Marc. Cool down quickly in an ice bath (a large bowl filled with ice cubes is fine), then leave in the fridge overnight. Churn in an ice-cream machine.

SPICED ICE CREAM

Makes 2 litres

1 litre double cream

1 litre full-fat milk

1 cinnamon stick,
broken in half

2 cloves, crushed

3 allspice berries

2 star anise

½ nutmeg

2 cardamom pods,
crushed

½ tsp ground ginger

grated zest of 1 orange

grated zest of ½ lemon

10 egg yolks

500g caster sugar

2 tbsp ruby port

One of Justin's cheeky creations.

Place the cream, milk, spices and fruit zest in a plastic container and leave in the fridge for around 16 hours to infuse. Transfer to a saucepan and bring slowly to the boil. Meanwhile, place the egg yolks and sugar in a large bowl and whisk together for a couple of minutes. Pour the boiling milk over the egg yolk mixture, whisking constantly to prevent curdling, then return the mixture to the saucepan. Cook over a low heat, stirring constantly with a wooden spoon, until it thickens enough to coat the back of the spoon.

Pour through a fine sieve into a plastic container and cool down quickly in an ice bath (a large bowl filled with ice cubes is fine). Stir in the port. Leave the mixture in the fridge overnight, then churn in an ice-cream machine.

BROWN BREAD AND ARMAGNAC ICE CREAM

Makes 1 litre

250g stale brown bread, crusts cut off

250g caster sugar

4 large egg yolks

600ml double cream

1½ tbsp Armagnac

It's amazing how stale brown bread becomes delicious frozen nuduals.

You will not need an ice-cream machine for this recipe.

Whizz up the bread in a food processor or blender to make crumbs, then spread them out on a baking sheet and toast in an oven preheated to 180°C/Gas Mark 4 until golden brown. Remove from the oven and leave overnight to dry out.

Put 75g of the sugar in a heavy-based saucepan with 2 tablespoons of water and place over a low heat until melted, tilting the pan occasionally so it melts evenly. Raise the heat and boil without stirring until a dark tan caramel is produced. Stir in the whizzed breadcrumbs and pour the mixture on to an oiled baking tray to cool and set. Blitz to coarse crumbs in a food processor and then put to one side.

Place the egg yolks and the remaining sugar in a large bowl and set it over a saucepan of simmering water, making sure the water is not touching the base of the bowl. Whisk with an electric beater until the mixture has tripled in volume and is very thick and glossy. Remove from the heat and leave to cool slightly.

Meanwhile, whisk the double cream until it forms soft peaks. When the egg yolk mix has cooled, fold in the whipped cream, then fold in the breadcrumbs, followed by the Armagnac. Pour into a plastic container and place in the freezer until set. It's great served with Hot Chocolate Sauce (see page 160).

DR HENDERSON ICE CREAM

Makes 1 litre

500ml full-fat milk

250ml double cream

7 large egg yolks

115g caster sugar

150ml Fernet Branca liqueur

40ml crème de menthe

A miracle in the form of ice cream.

Put the milk and cream into a heavy-based saucepan and slowly bring to the boil. Meanwhile, place the egg yolks and sugar in a large bowl and whisk together for a couple of minutes. Pour the boiling milk over the egg yolk mixture, whisking constantly to prevent curdling, then return the mixture to the saucepan. Cook over a low heat, stirring constantly with a wooden spoon, until it thickens enough to coat the back of the spoon. Remove from the heat and stir in the Fernet Branca and crème de menthe.

Pour through a fine sieve into a plastic container and cool down quickly in an ice bath (a large bowl filled with ice cubes is fine). Leave in the fridge overnight, then churn in an ice-cream machine.

HONEY AND BRANDY
ICE CREAM

Makes 1 litre

3 large eggs, separated

125g caster sugar

1½ tbsp pure clear honey

450ml double cream

90ml brandy

Buzzz buzzz.

You don't need an ice-cream machine for this. Basically you make it in three stages, all using an electric mixer with the whisk attachment.

First, whisk the egg yolks, sugar and honey together for 5 minutes on medium speed until pale and fluffy, then put to one side.

Secondly, whisk the cream and brandy together until the cream forms soft peaks, then set aside.

Finally, with a clean whisk, beat the egg whites until they form soft peaks.

With all three stages finished, transfer the egg yolk mixture into a bowl large enough to hold everything. Then fold a quarter of the cream through the egg yolk mix, followed by a quarter of the egg white. Carry on in this way until everything has been mixed together, then pour into a plastic container and freeze overnight.

BLACKCURRANT LEAF
ICE CREAM

Makes 1 litre

a handful of
blackcurrant leaves
(about 4 or 5)

375ml full-fat milk

450ml double cream

5 large egg yolks

160g caster sugar

A mysterious whisper of blackcurrant.

Rip the blackcurrant leaves and put them in a plastic container with the milk and cream. Leave in the fridge overnight to infuse.

The next day, pour the mixture into a heavy-based saucepan and bring to the boil. Meanwhile, place the egg yolks and sugar in a large bowl and whisk together for a couple of minutes. Pour the boiling milk over the egg yolk mixture, whisking constantly to prevent curdling, then return the mixture to the saucepan. Cook over a low heat, stirring constantly with a wooden spoon, until it thickens enough to coat the back of the spoon.

Pour through a fine sieve into a plastic container and cool down quickly in an ice bath (a large bowl filled with ice cubes is fine). Leave in the fridge overnight, then churn in an ice-cream machine.

LEMON SORBET

Makes 750ml

250g caster sugar

375ml water

5 unwaxed lemons

A glass of Russian vodka poured over this will lift everyone's spirits.

Place the sugar and 250ml of the water in a saucepan and bring slowly to the boil, stirring to dissolve the sugar. Simmer until the mixture is reduced to 375ml.

While the syrup is reducing, pare off the zest from the lemons with a vegetable peeler, leaving the white pith behind, then squeeze out the juice. Place the zest and juice in a plastic container, pour over the hot syrup and add the remaining water. Leave to cool, then place in the fridge overnight. Churn in an ice-cream machine.

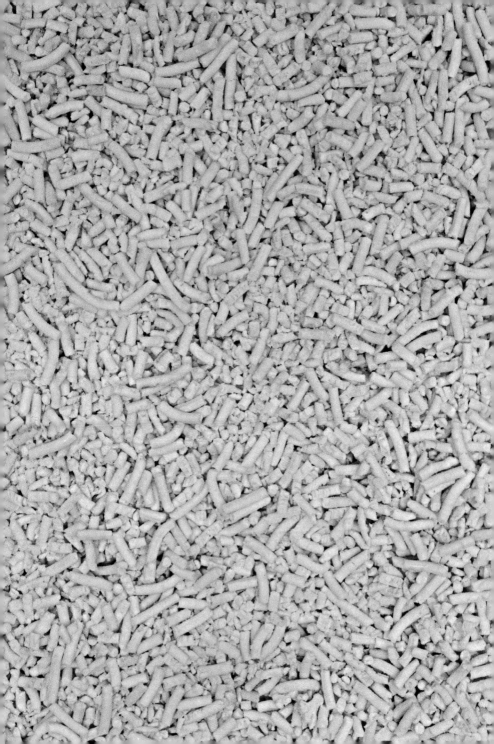

BASIC, BUT VITAL

MAKING A BRINE

Makes 4 litres

400g caster sugar

600g sea salt

12 juniper berries

12 cloves

12 black peppercorns

3 bay leaves

4 litres water

Bring all the brine ingredients together in a pot and bring to the boil so the sugar and salt melt. Decant into a container and allow to cool. When cold, add your meat. Leave it in the brine for the number of days required for your recipe.

TO CLARIFY BROTH

For 2 litres broth

450g raw lean flesh, from the same creature as your broth (this helps the flavour of your broth; the clarification might very slightly dent its flavour)

1 large or 2 small leeks, cleaned

2 egg whites and their shells

In a food processor, whizz the meat, leeks and egg whites and shells into a pulp. Whisk this mixture into your cold (preferably fridge cold) broth in a pan, place on the heat and bring to a gentle simmer. Do not stir again. What will be happening is similar to making coffee in a cafetière, but in reverse. The meat and egg form a sieve layer, which will rise through the broth, collecting any detritus on its way, until it forms a crust on top of the broth. This is why the most gentle of simmering is required, otherwise the crust will break up and be boiled back into the broth.

Once the crust has become reasonably firm, keep the pan on a gentle heat, otherwise the crust will sink, and lift it off with a slotted spoon. Finally, if your broth is not clear, then complete the process by straining it through muslin or a very fine sieve.

VINAIGRETTE

Makes approximately 300ml

2 *cloves of garlic, peeled*

1 *tbsp Dijon mustard*

*a pinch of sea salt
and black pepper*

juice of 1 lemon

2 *tsp white wine vinegar*

300*ml extra virgin
olive oil*

Crush the garlic (making sure this is finely done, as you don't want chips of garlic in your dressing). Add the mustard, salt and pepper, lemon juice and vinegar, then, as you mix, slowly add the olive oil so you get an emulsion. Once all the oil has been added, check the dressing for taste; you can add more salt and pepper, lemon juice or vinegar at this point.

The lemon juice and vinegar used together seem to set each other off, avoiding a too bitter lemon result, and the juice tempers the vinegar rather in the same magical way whiskey and lemon juice meet in a whiskey sour, both becoming something else altogether. This keeps very well in the fridge.

GREEN SAUCE

Makes plenty for 6

½ *bunch of*
curly parsley

½ *bunch of*
flat-leaf parsley

½ *bunch of mint*

¼ *bunch of dill*

a small showing of
tarragon (it has a habit
of taking over if added in
too large quantities)

1 *small tin of anchovy*
fillets, finely chopped

12 *cloves of garlic,*
peeled and finely
chopped

a handful of capers,
roughly chopped (if
extra-fine, keep whole)

extra virgin olive oil

crushed black pepper

Chop your herbs finely, but not too finely, and mix with the anchovies, garlic and capers. Add enough olive oil to give a loose, still spoonable, but not runny or oily consistency. Taste and season with black pepper (the anchovies should negate any necessity for salt).

PICKLED SHALLOTS

For 1kg shallots

sea salt

malt vinegar

white wine vinegar

8 cloves

10 allspice berries

2 cinnamon sticks

8 white peppercorns

10 black peppercorns

4 bay leaves

12 coriander seeds

4 small, hot dried chillies

Peel the shallots, then cover them with brine (made with 500g salt to 1.5 litres of water) and leave to soak in a plastic, glass or china container in the fridge for a week.

Now you know how much liquid it takes to cover your shallots, heat the same amount of a mixture of half and half malt vinegar and white wine vinegar in a stainless-steel pan with the collection of spices. While this comes to a simmer, rinse the shallots thoroughly. Place them in the simmering spiced vinegar for 5 minutes. Remove from the heat and bottle in sterilised sealable jars. Keep somewhere cool for a month. They are now ready to use. The leftover spiced vinegar is very good for dipping cooked whelks in.

CONVERSION TABLES

These are practical conversions for use in the kitchen. Dry spoon measures are rounded or heaped, not level.

DRY MEASURE

Metric	Imperial	Metric	Imperial
15 g	½ oz	250 g	9 oz
20 g	¾ oz	280 g	10 oz
30 g	1 oz	400 g	14 oz
55 g	2 oz	450 g	1 lb
100 g	3 ½ oz	500 g	1 lb 2 oz
150 g	5 oz	1 kg	2 lb 2 oz
175 g	6 oz	2 kg	4 lb 4 oz

FLOUR
100g = ¾ cup minus ½ tablespoon

CASTER SUGAR
100 g = ½ cup

BUTTER, CHEESE AND OTHER SOLIDS
100g = ½ cup minus 1 tablespoon

LIQUID MEASURE

Metric	US	fl oz
5 ml	1 tsp	
20 ml	1 tbsp	
25 ml	1½ tbsp	1 fl oz
50 ml	3 tbsp	2 fl oz
75 ml	4 tbsp	3 fl oz
100 ml	6 tbsp	4 fl oz
150 ml	½ cup	5 fl oz
300 ml	1¼ cups	10 fl oz
450 ml	2 cups	15 fl oz
575 ml	2½ cups	20 fl oz
700 ml	3 cups	25 fl oz
850 ml	3¾ cups	30 fl oz
1 litre	4 cups	35 fl oz

OVEN TEMPERATURES

Description	°C	°F	Gas Mark
very cool	110	225	¼
	120	250	½
cool	140	275	1
	150	300	2
gentle	160	325	3
medium	180	350	4
fairly hot	190	375	5
	200	400	6
hot	220	425	7
very hot	230	450	8
	240	475	9

LENGTHS

INDEX

218

burnt sheep's milk
yoghurt 166
butterscotch sauce 177

C
cabbage
   beetroot, red onion,
      red cabbage, crème
      fraîche and chervil
      salad 24
   guinea fowl, red cabbage,
      trotter and prune 47
   white cabbage and brown
      shrimp salad 26
cakes
   Eccles cakes 121
   madeleines 116
   prune loaf 113
   rhubarb crumble cake 157
   seed cake 108
Calvados
   apple and Calvados
      trifle 146–7
Campari and white wine 3
caramel 193
cauliflower
   butter bean, leek and
      cauliflower salad 22
cheese
   baked goat's curd
      cheesecake 168
   fennel and Berkswell 82
   Wigmore and potato
      pie 80–1

cheesecake,
   baked goat's curd 168
chervil
   beetroot, red onion,
      red cabbage, crème
      fraîche and chervil
      salad 24
chicken and ox tongue
   pie 56–7
chickpeas
   snail, trotter, sausage
      and chickpeas 51
chocolate
   bitter chocolate cream 142
   chocolate baked
      Alaska 136–7
   chocolate custard 126
   chocolate ice cream 192–3
   hot chocolate pudding 135
   hot chocolate sauce 160–1
   little chocolate buns 109
confit pig's cheek and
   dandelion 32–3
court-bouillon 58
crème fraîche
   beetroot, red onion,
      red cabbage, crème
      fraîche and chervil
      salad 24
   spinach, Dijon mustard
      and crème fraîche 65
crème pâtissière 124
crumble mix 157
custard 146
   chocolate custard 126

rice pudding with marc
   and raisin custard 164–5

D
damson jelly 143
dandelion leaves
   confit pig's cheek and
      dandelion 32–3
dates
   sticky date pudding 178–9
Dr Henderson ice cream 200
doughnuts 122–3

E
Earl Grey tea,
   Agen prunes in 134
Eccles cakes 121
eggs
   bacon, egg and bean
      salad 20

F
fennel
   fennel and Berkswell 82
   fennel, butter bean, ox
      tongue and green sauce
      soup 12–13
   grey mullet,
      fennel twigs and
      Jerusalem artichokes 68
fish
   grey mullet,
      fennel twigs and
      Jerusalem artichokes 68
   grilled mackerel 67

219

ACKNOWLEDGEMENTS

FH

Thank you to all, past and present, at St. John and St. John Bread and Wine.

JPG

Thank you to Fergus Henderson, Trevor Gulliver, Peter Harrison, Philip Crowther, Karl Goward, Paul Merrett, Kitty Travers, Ed Lewis, and all at St. John and St. John Bread and Wine – especially Cau, Abbey and Susan.